BAJA TO BARROW

BAJA TO BARROW

A PACIFIC COAST WILDLIFE ODYSSEY

Photographs and text by
Erwin and Peggy Bauer

Willow Creek Press

Minocqua, Wisconsin

© 1995 Willow Creek Press
All photographs © Erwin and Peggy Bauer except: page 7, Jeff
Foott/Tom Stack & Associates; page 106, Thomas Kitchin/Tom
Stack & Associates; and page 157, Bob Mauch.

ISBN 1-57223-022-3

Published by Willow Creek Press
               an imprint of Outlook Publishing
               P.O. Box 147
               Minocqua, WI 54548

Designed by Patricia Bickner Linder

For information on other Willow Creek titles,
write or call 1-800-850-9453.

Printed in Hong Kong.

Library of Congress Cataloguing-in-Publication Data

Bauer, Erwin A.
     Baja to Barrow : a Pacific Coast wildlife odyssey / photographs
and text by Erwin and Peggy Bauer.
     p.   cm.
     ISBN 1-57223-022-3 (hardcover)
     1. Natural history–Pacific Coast (North America)–Guidebooks.
2. Pacific Coast (North America)–Guidebooks.   I. Bauer, Peggy.
II. Title.
QH104.5.P32B38   1995
     508.79–dc20   95-7007
                                                       CIP

Table of Contents

Introduction

Late every summer, after gorging on the rich bounty of the Bering Sea, most of the world's surviving gray whales suddenly become restless. They gather in shallow waters. Their otherwise active feeding activities stop. Then just as the gray-green Alaskan tundra shores are turning to red and gold, about 11,000 of these whales, the world's largest living creatures, begin the longest migration made by any mammals on earth.

Throughout fall, and strung out for more than a hundred miles, the whales cruise southward through Bristol Bay and past the first landfall at Izembek Lagoon, where vast, dark flocks of brant are testing their wings before beginning a similar journey. Led by pregnant cows, the whales enter the north Pacific Ocean through a narrow pass between Unimak Island and the western tip of the Alaskan Peninsula. From here they turn south-southeastward. Using some mystical navigation system we still do not understand, and traveling about four miles per hour, day and night, most of the whales pass northern British Columbia between Thanksgiving and Christmas. Hugging the coasts of Washington, Oregon and California much of the way, they arrive off Baja California, Mexico, in early January.

Although some calves are born just north of the Mexican border before the travelers reach their traditional "calving grounds," most of the 14-foot-long young begin life in the warm, calm bays of Baja California between mid-January and early February, as they have for thousands of years and generations. After the young are born, mating takes place. This is the most turbulent time of the adult whales' lives. By the end of May, their passion spent, the adult whales, accompanied by their calves, will be traveling back along the coast to spend the summer in the Bering Sea. The round trip covers about 7,000 miles.

More important than distance is the route of the great whales. It parallels, and at many points is within sight of, the most magnificent coastline on the face of this planet. Now, near the end of the 20th century, no other stretch of seashore anywhere supports so much wildlife—so many species in such nearly incalculable numbers—as this one extending from the tip of Baja to Barrow, Alaska. In centuries past there may have been other shores on other continents similarly endowed, but no longer.

► Gray whale off the coast of British Columbia.

Even without the wildlife, this is also the most spectacularly scenic of the world's coasts, from the tan, hot deserts of Baja to the bleak Arctic flats at Barrow. It is true that too much of the original natural beauty is buried beneath human development; about 80 percent of the people living in our coastal states are concentrated within 50 miles of the ocean. Some of the original wildlife residents, for example the California condor and the California grizzly, are gone forever. The condor today lives only in captivity. Too many coastal forests have been clear-cut with no thought whatever to sustainable use or the future. The Exxon oil spill near Valdez, Alaska, has proved to be a far greater, longer-lasting tragedy than anyone believed. But enough of the awesome beauty of our Pacific Coast is still intact and it is easy to explore. Most of the wild native animals, from frogs to flycatchers, sea otters to sea lions, and black-tailed deer to brown bears, are still there to be seen.

During the past 20 years, my wife Peggy and I have been lucky enough to follow exactly the route of the gray whales from where it seldom rains to where it always (or so it sometimes seems) rains. We have traveled by land and sea, but without the whales' biological clocks ticking, without the tides and ocean currents working against us. Between these trips from Baja to Barrow and back we have detoured to other coastlines around the world and, except for Antarctica, none come close to our Pacific shore for diversity, stunning beauty and inspiration. This book is about some of our adventures, always with cameras in hand.

A harem of stellar sea lions, Kenai Fjords National Park, Alaska.

▼

► Brown pelican on a southern California beach.

◄ Tufted puffin, Oregon.

► ► Overleaf: Cormorants and brown pelicans rest as the tide changes off Cabo San Lucas in the Gulf of California.

Baja

Visible from mainland Mexico on clear days, and isolated by the Gulf of California, or Sea of Cortez, a thin sliver of stark, arid real estate unlike any other simmers under a hot sun. It is Baja (Spanish for under or beneath) California, shaped roughly like a thin, gnarled finger, 800 miles long and averaging only 40 miles wide. It points southeastward from the southern border of the state of California into the Pacific Ocean.

Photographs taken daily by robot cameras in weather satellites orbiting far overhead show a land relatively unpopulated and unspoiled by human ambition. Its central mountain range, deep canyons, hot deserts, spectacular beaches and uninhabited offshore islands are never obscured by smog and are only rarely in the shadow of thin clouds. A satellite view of Baja suggests nothing less than a lost paradise.

What the satellite cameras cannot reveal are the unique flora and fauna that live in this dry Eden. Eighty of the 120 different species of cacti catalogued so far grow nowhere else. These range in size from one smaller than a thumbnail to the giant cardon. One cardon cactus near Bahia de los Angeles stands more than 60 feet tall and probably weighs 12 tons. Another large plant is the grotesque boojum tree that almost defies classification but in shape resembles an inverted carrot. It exists nowhere else but Baja.

ENSENADA

Isla Cedros

Bahia Sebastian Viscaino

Bahia Asuncion

GULF OF CALIFORNIA

Cabo San Lazaro

Isla Santa Margarita

Isla del Espiritu Sa

LA PAZ

CABO SAN LUCAS

► Great blue herons court beside a lonely Baja lagoon.

The peninsula is home to a kangaroo mouse that never drinks water in its life, a bat
that seeks fish, seabirds that nest underground or atop spiny cacti, and rattlesnakes
without rattles. Desert bighorn sheep haunt the highest, driest ridges of the Sierra de
la Gigante, and distinct, dark races of mule deer and jackrabbits survive on islands in
the Gulf of California where rain seldom falls. I read avidly about this mysterious place when still a
young man and knew I had to see it some day.

My opportunity came early in 1955 when I drove—or rather bounced and careened—the entire
length of Baja from Tijuana on the United States-Mexico border, where the pavement ended, south to
Cabo San Lucas with my friend Glenn Lau. Most of the territory then was roadless, even uncharted,
and some of the roads shown on our only map proved to be impassable. It was a rough, dusty, thirsty
trip in a tired old jeep that already had enough mileage on its odometer to indicate it had traveled
three times around the globe. The two of us camped at night, unrolling our sleeping bags on the
ground wherever night overtook us. We were lucky to make a hundred miles in a whole day's driving.
We built campfires of dead cactus trunks or driftwood and bathed in stock tanks only half-filled by
creaking, rusty windmills. One of the few other travelers we met was the photographer Eliot Porter,
who was making the first photo record of interior Baja. Although eventually most of our attention was

focused simply on completing the journey intact, I saw enough of the brooding landscapes and had enough tantalizing glimpses of the wildlife that I vowed to return.

Twenty years later I did go back, this time with my wife, Peggy, driving a pickup truck with lower mileage than the jeep had registered, and four-wheel-drive. The main peninsular road was improved, marginally, but it was still an uncertain, seat-of-the-pants adventure. This time we explored Baja from the bottom northward, by taking the weekly car ferry from Topolobampo on the Mexican mainland to La Paz, Baja, and then driving toward San Diego.

Despite the terrible, unmarked roads and being lost too much of the time, it was an extraordinary trip. We caught fish to eat wherever our meandering route touched saltwater and where we could camp alone on empty beaches. Since it was a springtime following heavier than normal winter rains, we passed through many areas where the wildflowers—poppies, iceplants and cacti—were in bloom. We added new birds to our life lists, Aplomado falcons and zone-tailed hawks among them.

At dusk one evening we camped in a rocky draw without inspecting the spot too carefully. As a result we were kept awake all night by the pitiful yipping and mournful wailing that seemed to emanate only a short distance from our rolled-up jacket pillows. At dawn we discovered the problem.

◄

An osprey perches on a giant cardon cactus.

▼

This rattleless rattlesnake is endemic to Isla San Lorenzo.

▲

A coyote pup peers from its den in the Baja desert.

We had inadvertently set up our tent almost on top of a den containing small coyote pups. What we had heard were the hungry puppies too afraid to come outside and the mother too frightened to bring them food. Other mornings rufous hummingbirds buzzed around our faces poking out of sleeping bags. Often, California quail foraging nearby would awaken us.

The last time we saw Baja was from an entirely different perspective and in far greater creature comfort. The *Lindblad Explorer*, a passenger vessel designed more for adventure cruising to the ends of the earth than for luxury (but still with far more comforts than we had experienced here before), scheduled a trip that would almost completely encircle Baja, and we were aboard. The *Explorer's* small fleet of inflatable Zodiac rafts made it possible to explore both the peninsula and its offshore islands, which are not accessible by any other means. In some places we left behind footprints where few if any other humans had walked before.

The cruise began in Acapulco in May and aimed northward toward Cabo San Lucas, which is Baja's land's end. Not far from shore we saw the first wildlife, a school of whale sharks, the largest fish that swim in any ocean, traveling on the surface. Spotted, and about six feet across their broad, blunt heads, some of these sharks were over 30 feet long. A school of much smaller hammerhead sharks seemed to be tracking them from below.

From the Zodiacs we explored at close range the arches and sea caves that are constantly battered by a powerful surf. At Cabo's tip we learned how the local sea lions are able to spend long days sunning on rock pinnacles high above the Pacific. At high tide, the sleek animals wait for the peaks

of ocean swells to lift and carry them up into place. No difficult climbing is necessary and they can doze in peace, safe from passing sharks and killer whales, at least until the next high tide.

From Cabo the *Explorer* turned northward into the sea of Cortez and anchored off Isla San Pedro Martir just before daybreak. The island's jagged volcanic profile was eerie in the sulfur light of pre-dawn. Peggy and I were among the first to wade ashore in the lukewarm surf, carrying backpacks heavy with cameras, drinking water and film.

Once ashore, San Pedro seemed even more surreal in the sunrise than it had from the ship. The island is nearly conical, about a mile in diameter, with steep slopes that climb to a single peak about 1,500 feet above the beach. Except for a climax forest of huge cardon cactus, few other plants of any kind grow here. Most of the cardons are crusted with white, and we soon saw why: as we walked slowly about, the forest came alive with nesting, perching and defecating seabirds.

Western gulls were nesting closest to the rocky shoreline. Red-billed tropic birds were incubating eggs or tending chicks in dark crevices just above the gulls. Climbing farther up the guano-whitened

slopes, we came upon more and more nesting birds, brown- and blue-footed boobies mixed among larger numbers of brown pelicans. At first we could sense a slight nervousness among the birds as we approached, so we stopped and sat motionless awhile, studying the remarkable scene. Soon the nesters no longer even looked at us. When pairs of blue-footed boobies began coursing by, sky-pointing and whistling softly only a few feet away, we dug the cameras from our backpacks and began shooting.

▼
This blue-footed booby and its chick are nesting on a small Gulf island.

▲
Snowy egrets are commonly seen fishing in Baja lagoons.

◄
The giant cardon cactus is often almost the only plant on some Gulf islands.

Altogether, 15 species of marine birds nest on 15 islets such as San Pedro Martir in the Sea of Cortez, some in phenomenal numbers. Most abundant is the least storm petrel with half a million pairs. Elegant terns, Heermann's (red-billed) gulls and brown pelicans are believed to number about 350,000 pairs. The smaller and more isolated the islands, the more attractive they seem to be for nesting. Also, the needs of each species are different enough to keep competition at a minimum.

Later in the morning we circled San Pedro in the Zodiacs and found that some sections of the islands had been deeply undercut at sea level, forming large caverns in which several hundred copper-colored California sea lions basked in the sunshine. All of the animals looked up suspiciously at our approach, and some began barking nervously, but others barely opened their eyes. A few plunged into the water and swam part way out to meet us and follow for a short distance in the Zodiac's wake.

We could willingly have explored much longer in the Sea of Cortez, but had only ten days. Over time, nature photographers learn to live with good breaks and bad ones, with fair weather and foul, and so far this expedition was a good one all around.

Proceeding northward, the sometimes windy, turbulent sea was as smooth for us as a great oil slick. Landing on lonely islands was never a problem. Not far from the landing spot on Isla Estanque we found a colony of bats living in gloomy rock fissures. They flew out to forage after we departed and darkness had fallen. On Isla Angel de la Guarda's north end we had to detour hurriedly around

▲

Long-eared myotis passes daytimes in caves and crevices of some Baja/Gulf islands.

▲

This young osprey is almost ready to fly from its Raza Island nest.

beachmaster bull sea lions that challenged us, to reach high ground and have a look at nests of ospreys. Studying these from a distance through binoculars, we could see that some energetic, peripatetic birdbander had already been there. All of the chicks had numbered bands affixed to their legs. Before leaving Guarda, a parent osprey glided low overhead and dropped a fish into one of the nests. If the young had been worried about our presence, it didn't keep them from eating.

Hiking on small Isla San Lorenzo, we were fortunate to find one of the endemic rattlesnakes that is ringed in black and white on the end of its tail, but has no rattles. However, the snake still vibrated its bare tail in warning as other rattlers do. On nearby Isla Tortuga we discovered a small concentration of other rattlesnakes that were not aggressive and did not try to escape from us. These were a subspecies of the western diamond-back rattler that is fairly common—and more irritable—on the Mexican mainland.

Cruising between San Lorenzo and Tortuga we passed among a pod of false killer whales, which are world travelers, and nearby a pod of finback, or fin, whales. The latter probably spend their entire lives in the Gulf of California.

Nowhere on our *Explorer* trip did we have a glimpse of vaquitas, the small dolphins of the Gulf of California that are probably the most endangered sea mammals in the world. They are also the smallest of all cetaceans and were not really "discovered" until 1950. Perhaps never really abundant, vaquitas have been rendered nearly extinct in the northern Gulf by the reduced flow of the Colorado River (due to the many dams along its course) and by commercial overfishing of totuavas, a mainstay in the dolphins' diet that were once very abundant. Today totuavas are also considered endangered. It is possible that the last vaquitas seen alive were a mother and calf videotaped near Rocas Consag in the northern Gulf in 1991 by Vicki Monks, an investigative reporter for Defenders of Wildlife, a conservation activist group.

Of all the Gulf of California islands, Raza may be the most fantastic, especially if approached as we did during an exploding sunrise. From our anchorage offshore, the tiny island seemed to be belching birds into the sky. After wading ashore and climbing over a low rock barrier, we followed a faint trail

toward a growing din of birds. Soon we could see that nearly all were elegant and royal terns, with fewer Heermann's gulls.

We estimated about 40,000 terns nested in one vast rookery at the center of the island on a flat, bare depression. Compressed almost wing to wing, the terns engaged in a noisy, seething turmoil of bickering and brooding while feeding fluffy, recently hatched young. Above and all around this mass of white feathers, black heads and orange bills, the gulls patrolled, ready to pounce on any tern chick that wandered away or was left unguarded for an instant. Survival of the fittest (or luckiest?) was taking place on a grand scale in front of our telephoto lenses.

Looking for a more distant and higher vantage point from which to photograph the entire tern rookery, I used handholds and precarious footholds to climb onto a steep rock pile overlooking the nesting melee on one side and the Gulf on the other. Reaching the top I almost stepped into an osprey nest. Two nearly full-grown chicks inside had crouched low and unseen until I loomed almost directly above them. Now I could see them squawking and hissing at me. I stayed near the nest long enough to notice both these chicks had also been banded. It is interesting to note that, elsewhere, ospreys nest in trees, but on Baja most nests are on the ground, and a few are found in cardon cacti.

After a week in the Gulf of California, the *Explorer* rounded Cabo San Lucas and proceeded northward again along Baja's Pacific coast, escorted by petrels, dusky, Manx and pink-footed

▲

Black-crowned night herons are often
seen at San Quintin Bay.

◀

A marbled godwit probes the edge of a
lagoon along the Pacific coast at dusk.

shearwaters and a lone black-footed albatross. We did not stop at Laguna San Ignacio, Ojo de Liebre (Scammon's Lagoon) or Guerrero Negro, which the calving and breeding gray whales had deserted to return to the Bering Sea only a month earlier. But we did pause at Isla Cedros and San Benito, midway up the peninsula.

On the first island, Cedros, we hiked over wild beaches where California sea lions proved too shy to be photographed. A few had newborn pups, and that may have been the reason. Instead we climbed up into flat-bottomed gravel washes that have known severe and sudden runoffs. In one wash we found the golden barrel cactus endemic to Cedros and in another found the first sweet water seep on any of the Baja islands. The clear, warm trickle disappeared underground long before it could reach the ocean. Tracks etched in soft spots around this fresh water provided evidence that the endemic mule deer had stopped here to drink.

On the first cloudy, threatening day of the entire voyage, the Zodiacs carried us to a beachhead on San Benito island. Although a long list of birds (pelicans, snowy egrets, horned larks, black-crowned night herons, black petrels, common and California gulls, cormorants, American oystercatchers, Cassin's auklets and Xantus' murrelets) commute or nest here among the 50 or so resident Mexicans engaged in collecting abalones, San Benito really belongs to a mammal that one passenger described as a moldy, two-and-one-half-ton sausage that has been in storage too long. She meant the northern elephant seal, many of which happened to be shedding—molting—on the beach when we arrived.

The northern elephant is a true seal, the largest member of the seal family, and may weigh almost twice as much as a Pacific walrus. Mature bulls can reach two and a half tons and measure 17 feet long.

Cows average less than half that size. Young ones are born black but eventually take on the slate-gray to brownish color of adults. All shed their outer coat semiannually; it peels off in large patches, giving the animal an unhealthy and unattractive appearance. When the shedding is complete the seals are again dark brown and velvety, especially when wet.

We arrived at San Benito too late for the elephant seals' mating season. During that period, for as long as a month, the male elephant seals spend almost all their time intimidating and battling one another for possession of harems containing as many as 50 females. If another male approaches, the harem bull charges, moving like a huge demented inchworm, rising on its haunches, inflating its huge nose (which serves as a resonating chamber), throwing back its head and roaring loud enough to be heard for a long distance. If that doesn't drive off the contender, the bull slams the intruder with its chest and neck and attacks with its sharp canine teeth. Blood flows. As a result, most veterans of the mating wars carry battle scars, especially on the neck. So violent does the fighting sometimes become

A young elephant seal surfaces near San Benito Island.

that newborn pups in the path of the battlers are often crushed. Theirs is a hierarchal breeding system in which only about one in ten bulls ever earns the "rights" to reproduce. Actual mating takes place soon after the cows give birth to single pups, and the reproductive act cannot be described as a tender or romantic interlude: when copulating, the bull mounts and holds down the much smaller cow by gripping her neck in his jaws.

If the elephant seal is conspicuous during its winter mating season, until recently its whereabouts for the rest of the year have been a mystery. The herds seemed to simply disappear at sea. But new studies with time-depth recorders attached to a few individuals from Año Nuevo State Park, California, have revealed an extraordinary lifestyle. During their time at sea the animals dive and feed on the ocean floor almost nonstop. Dives of between 1,000 and 2,000 feet are not uncommon, and elephant seals make such dives over and over, with little rest in between. They stay down about 20 minutes per dive but are capable of remaining submerged for an hour. Marine biologists have recorded dives by two seals, one bull, one cow, of nearly a mile. That is the deepest dive by any sea mammal, by any air-breathing vertebrate (including the sperm whale, once considered the champion diver) known to science.

The elephant seal's deep-diving ability is an important advantage: it allows the animal to feed in extreme ocean depths where few if any other animals compete for squid, Pacific whiting and other bioluminescent prey. The seal's large, beautiful eyes must be helpful in finding prey in the dark depths of the sea.

A foraging expedition may cover thousands of miles and take the elephant seals of San Benito (and elsewhere along the California coast) as far as Alaska and Hawaii. Somehow they unerringly find their way back to "home beaches," where, when not mating, large groups snooze motionless, in a torpor, which is when and how most people see them. It is this inactivity, plus a lack of fear of humans, that almost pushed northern elephant seals over the edge into extinction late in the last century.

Sealers especially prized this marine mammal for its blubber; that of a large bull will render 90 gallons of valuable oil. But sealing decimated northern elephant seal herds. Eventually only about 100 survived on one island, Guadalupe, mostly because sealers never found them at this remote spot 150 miles west of Baja California. Just in time, the Mexican and United States governments acted to protect the Guadalupe survivors, which have since almost miraculously multiplied. Today about 15,000 elephant seals live on Guadalupe, and an additional dozen island rookeries exist along the Pacific Coast from San Benito northward to Point Reyes National Seashore near San Francisco. With former predators such as grizzly bears and wolves only a long-ago memory, in the late 1950s, the elephant seals began to haul out and breed on the

Seabirds use ledges of this Ildefonso shore rock as nesting and roosting sites.

▼

California mainland at Año Nuevo State Park.

We spent a wild and uncomfortable night as the *Explorer* bucked gale force winds and heavy seas, cruising northwestward from San Benito toward Guadalupe Island. Our cabin was so far forward and susceptible to the ship's roll, that I slept, or tried to, on a bed of deck pads in the library near midships. Shortly after daybreak we arrived just off the sheltered east shore and moved slowly north within sight of land. Very soon we saw 25 Guadalupe fur seals on rocky ground at the base of a steep cliff. Farther along we spotted more and still more until Zodiacs were lowered to try to get a closer look at them. We did motor to within about 50 yards of an angry surf, but this was far too rough for photography or even for such a small craft to maneuver safely. Very soon we were forced to retreat to the *Explorer*. It was difficult winching the Zodiacs back on board; a crewman was injured in the process.

Once, untold thousands of the Guadalupe species of fur seals lived exclusively on this steep volcanic landfall. But like pinnipeds around the world, they were harvested during the 19th century for furs and oil, without regard to the future. By about 1894 the last known individuals were killed by Russian sealers who brought experienced Aleuts from Alaska to do the sealing. (Later, when the weather calmed, we walked on shore among the ruins of the sealers' stone huts.) Scientists did not even have a chance to examine this species or to name it before all were apparently gone. Thus, both the elephant seal and fur seal populations were nearly obliterated from the Pacific coast. The fact that they survived at all was not due to any thoughts about conservation, but because of an oversight on the part of the hunters.

In 1949 a single male fur seal appeared on San Nicolas in the California Channel Islands. Five years later a biological expedition to Guadalupe led by Carl Hubbs found a small breeding colony in an isolated sea cave. Somehow these few had remained undiscovered and escaped the slaughter. Today the population of this rare seal is estimated at between 500 and 1,000, all but a handful living on Guadalupe, where sleek black pups are born in or near deep caves and recesses in the rocks each June.

We spent another day exploring Guadalupe on foot, but, except for the sea mammals

▲

Coral beans provide a splash of color in Baja's dry desert.

▲

California sea lions basking on rocky shore ledges.

◄

A California sea lion stares back at photographers passing its Baja haulout.

living around the edges, it was not an enchanting place. The island was overrun with a scourge of feral goats that survive by destroying whatever is left of the Bishop pines and other native vegetation, drinking only dew water for moisture. We climbed a switchbacked trail built long ago by Mexican convicts and used by abalone collectors who occasionally hunt the goats for meat while waiting out Pacific storms. Another gale and drenching rain kept us from reaching the strange island's summit, about 4,000 feet above sea level.

The next day, our last on the *Explorer*, we moved northward, crossing into California, U.S.A., and docking in Los Angeles. All the while we were planning another trip to Baja.

We did return late one January on a trip that almost anybody in southern California could duplicate on a long weekend. From San Diego it is a fairly easy five-hour drive southward on Baja Route One to the town of Lazaro Cardenas, and then west to San Quintin Bay, which is one of a few remaining undisturbed Pacific Coast estuaries. In fact, it is the only such estuary for about 1,000 miles between San Francisco and Scammon's Lagoon that has never been dredged. Waters of San Quintin Bay are still pure, free of sewage and other contaminants. So far, the coastal sand dunes have not been invaded by off-road vehicles and have not been subdivided for housing or resorts. In winter the bay area is a unique, undisturbed paradise. It looks like all of southern California must have looked before it was discovered by Europeans.

San Quintin is a Y-shaped bay of almost 30 square miles with vast tidal flats and beds of eelgrass. Pickleweed and cordgrass dominate the surrounding saltwater marshes on which only two or three inches of rain fall every 12 months. This rich estuarine habitat attracts birds in great variety and

► Roadrunners are also commonly seen in Baja California.

▼ Ruddy turnstones forage along the beach near San Quintin.

▲

Young bull elephant seals sparring near San Benito Island.

►

A great blue heron stalks the San Quintin shoreline at sunrise.

numbers from December until May. Crouched one morning along the northeast shore of the estuary at low tide, Peggy and I watched at one time in one area most of the waterfowl species that ever fly along the Pacific Coast. Most numerous were the rafts of black brant, but we also tallied large numbers of pintail, lesser scaup, redhead, surf scoter and widgeon. We were also surprised to see a few white-fronted geese and Aleutian Canada geese, the latter of which are uncommon and endangered. Some of the birds fed on tender eelgrass shoots while others probed in the mud for small invertebrates and other fare. We counted great blue herons and black-crowned night herons and common egrets. We also found a small great blue heron rookery in dead trees near the edge of the lagoon.

During extreme high tides we turned our attention from the ducks and geese to shorebirds. The high water level prevented them from searching the mudflats for food and instead concentrated them in a few dry areas within easy range of our spotting scopes. The most abundant were willets and marbled godwits, long- and short-billed dowitchers and least sandpipers. I believe it was one of the latter that a merlin speared and carried away more quickly —and more suddenly—than our eyes could follow. The number of bird species we listed at San Quintin was astonishing, including a single and secretive, endangered light-footed clapper rail. Pelicans, gulls, terns, herons, egrets and cormorants were everywhere, especially around an oyster aquaculture project in an area called False Bay. We also counted black skimmers, a species that has only recently appeared in Baja California.

San Quintin has something else likely to convince ecotravelers to linger: the Molino Viejo (or Old Mill) Motel. It is not a luxury lodging, but it is tidy, and we found that birding is spoken in both Spanish and English. Some of the best birding areas are only a short hike or drive away.

California

The Really Golden State

today it is almost impossible to conceive that grizzly bears, great numbers of grizzly bears, once stalked the California coast, where one large metropolis now blends into the next and little open space, let alone wilderness, exists.

The first mention of California's grizzly bears comes from Sebastian Vizcaino, who landed with a party near Monterey in 1602 and found many of the bears feeding on a whale that had washed ashore. They resented his intrusion. Grizzlies were at the top of the food chain from Mexico to Oregon (and in fact the entire state of California) when the first Spanish explorers and settlers arrived. The bruins were most numerous in exactly those regions of southern California most densely populated by people in the 20th century.

In 1769 Gaspar de Portola, leading an expedition near San Luis Obispo, reported seeing "troops of bears" and vast areas of land plowed up where the animals had been grubbing for roots. In the same area in 1803, two other men reported seeing 18 grizzlies in one afternoon, "not all of them friendly." One hundred years later, John Xantus would write to the Secretary of the Smithsonian Institution in Washington, D.C.: "We have here grislys in great abundance, they are really a nuisance, you cannot walk out half a mile without meeting some of them, and as they just now have their cubs, they are extremely ferocious so, I was already twice driven up a tree . . . "

Redwood National Park

EUREKA

Sonoma Coast State Beach

Pt. Reyes National Seashore

SAN FRANCISCO

Año Nuevo S.P.

SANTA CRUZ

MONTEREY
Point Lobos

Big Sur S.P.

SAN LUIS OBISPO

Montana de Oro S.P.

SANTA BARBARA

San Miguel I.

Santa Cruz I.

Santa Rosa Island

REDONDO BEACH

Channel Islands N. P.

Santa Catalina Island

San Clemente Island

SAN DIEGO

► Sonoma Coast — Less than two centuries ago grizzly bears hunted along this splendid coastline in central California.

In 1814 an early rancher in Ventura County wrote that grizzly bears were "like herds of swine, always hungry." When food supplies were plentiful in a given area, a hundred or more might concentrate to take advantage of the bounty, similar to the way brown bears gather on Alaskan rivers during salmon spawning. Of course, the California bears were shot in wholesale numbers because grizzlies and cattle ranching are less than compatible. In many communities, men were known and respected for the number of bears they had dispatched. To shoot 200 in a single year was not unusual. A team of three hunters in the Tejon Pass area killed 150 in a few months.

As recently as 1845, Benjamin D. Wilson, who would soon be the first mayor of Los Angeles, set off on a punitive expedition against troublesome Mojave Indians. But his vaqueros were distracted by the many bears they found in a valley en route to San Bernardino. They roped 11 one day (to be used in bull-and-bear fights that were California versions of the traditional Spanish bullfights) and 11 more a couple of days later. "The whole swamp seemed alive with bear," Wilson wrote, naming the location Bear Valley. He never caught up with the Indians.

Ramon Ortega claimed that he counted 100 bears between Mission San Buenaventura and his

Rancho Sespe, which was near one of the last known strongholds of wild California condors.

The last grizzly, a species that had lived in California for a million years, was shot in 1922, reason unknown, by a first-generation rancher. There are only a few mounted museum specimens and fading photographs, as well as an image on the state flag, to remind us that grizzly bears once thrived here.

The last California condors were taken from the wild in 1990 to be used in captive breeding programs, with the aim of eventually reestablishing the species in the wild. In addition, a small number are living in California zoos.

If judged by the fate of the grizzly and condor alone, California would seem a place to quickly pass over on the way from Baja to Barrow in search of wildlife. But as I write, the conservation ethic is alive in the state. As headquarters of the Sierra Club and other active environmental groups not so well known, it just may be the most environmentally progressive place in America. That's fortunate because, next to Alaska, California may have the most to preserve.

Consider first the Channel Islands National Park, accurately described as a primitive anachronism in southern California's teeming megalopolis. The quarter-million-acre area comprises a fleet of five islands (three other islands are not included in the park) in the Pacific Ocean off Ventura County. The islands are near enough to be easily seen from the mainland on clear days. It is even possible to identify the bright yellow of giant coreopsis blooming briefly in springtime on Anacapa, the closest island. All the islands are products of their own climates, which can be much different than that of the mainland. At any time, clouds and mists can completely smother the islands, obliterating them from view.

A canvasback duck rests on a southern California coastal pond.

▼

Montana de Oro State Park.

▼

▲

Great blue herons nest in rookery near the coast in southern California.

Farthest south in the island group is 640-acre Santa Barbara Island, surrounded by cliffs and difficult to access. Anacapa is the nearest and most often visited, being only about 11 miles west of mainland Point Hueneme. Its shores also are steep and difficult, but one beach at Frenchy's Cove gives access to tour boat passengers from Ventura. Santa Cruz, 62,000 acres in size, is the largest of the Channel Islands. Its central peaks (to 2,400 feet)—especially those to the north, which are continuously pounded by prevailing winds—and great sea caves give it the most diverse topography of all. Santa Rosa is almost as large and its terrain is similar to that of Santa Cruz.

For me, the most interesting island by far is 10,000-acre San Miguel. In the past it was virtually denuded by livestock overgrazing; deeply eroded, bare ravines are the result. The island seems a magnet for unusually rough seas. At times it is drenched by fog for days on end. Add to this dreary scene the strange, whitened caliche "ghost forests" that "grow" in places on the San Miguel landscape. These formed when calcium carbonate was deposited on ancient trees very long ago. When the trees died and decayed, the weird shapes, eroded by wind and rain, were left behind. A first-time visitor might very well regard this as a hostile place.

All of the islands support unique and interesting wildlife populations. Six separate subspecies of the island fox, a gray fox smaller and less shy than that on the mainland, live on six islands. A nocturnal spotted skunk lives on Santa Rosa and Santa Cruz, which also has its own large scrub jay. All eight islands have their own subspecies of deer mouse, but San Miguel is the most astonishing wildlife island in the group.

Six kinds of seals have been seen on San Miguel: California and Steller's sea lions, northern elephant seals, harbor seals, and northern and Guadalupe fur seals. Five of these species breed here, making this the most diversified seal rookery on earth.

Early each spring, thousands of California sea lions arrive off Point Bennett, and then the beaches are jammed with sleek, bellowing bodies jockeying for space. The first pups are born in May at about the same time the males begin to battle for breeding territories and for females, the more of each the better. Breeding continues through the summer, but regardless of the date of conception, the next year's crop of pups will all be born at roughly the same time. Delayed implantation postpones gestation in all of the females until September.

Scientists believe that because California sea lions (and other pinnipeds) must bear their young on shore where they are vulnerable, there is greater safety in the large numbers that occur when all the pups are born at the same time. Mothers then have the remainder of the summer, with its generally milder weather, abundant food and fewer ocean storms, to rear the pups.

▲
A subspecies of spotted skunk lives in the Channel Islands National Park.

▼
An old northern elephant seal bull rests, exhausted after breeding season at Año Nuevo State Park.

California sea lion bulls may measure nine feet from nose to tail and weigh nearly a half ton. Fully grown cows measure up to six feet and weigh 300 pounds. This is the species that seems to thrive best in captivity and can so easily be trained to perform amazing feats of balance for seal shows in zoos and wildlife theme parks. The almost twice as large Steller's sea lion is not so easily tamed.

All of the pinnipeds (fin-footed mammals) everywhere are divided into two categories: eared seals (sea lions and fur seals) and true seals (harbor and elephant seals). The ears of eared seals are easily visible. Eared seals use their foreflippers when swimming and a waddling gait to move on shore. True seals, without external ears, scull with their hind flippers in the sea and slide on their bellies across the ground in a lunging motion. Neither type of seal is very adept at travel on land, but I have been surprised at how quickly a bull in the breeding season can move to defend a domain against a rival bull . . . or an incautious human who happens by.

The Channel Islands, Especially San Miguel, are major seabird rookeries of the eastern North Pacific. The offshore waters of the cold California Current flow southward, and its waters are rich enough in nutrients to feed many thousands of nesters. A list of these would include pigeon guillemots (which build nests on ledges and in cliff caves), western gulls, Brandt's cormorants, most of southern California's Cassin's auklets, storm petrels, black oystercatchers, snowy plovers and Xantus' murrelet. San Miguel is the northernmost nesting grounds of the Xantus'.

Midway through the 20th century, 5,000 pairs of California brown pelicans nested on Anacapa Island alone. By 1968 there were only 100 pairs, with none on the other Channel Islands, and no young pelicans were produced. However, the Anacapa colony was littered with broken egg shells. The cause: a DDT manufacturer had dumped factory wastes into the ocean, and that pesticide accumulated in aquatic plants, fish, and ultimately in the pelicans. The nesters laid eggs, but the shells were too thin to support the weight of the incubating adults. Thus the California race of pelican seemed likely to join the grizzly and condor in oblivion.

None too soon for humans as well as the California pelicans, DDT was banned

◄ A California sea lion wonders if the cameraman has come too close.

▼ Young elephant seal bulls spar in a brackish pond at Año Nuevo State Park.

in the United States in 1972. In the next few years the big birds began a slow recovery, and by 1980 the Channel Islands breeding population was almost back to its original level.

We have enjoyed watching and photographing wildlife at a number of places along the coast of southern California. Among the most memorable is the Tijuana Slough National Estuarine Reserve, the largest estuarine wetland in the region, and nearby Sweetwater Marsh National Wildlife Refuge (hereinafter NWR) near Imperial Beach, for many species of wading and shorebirds, California ground squirrels, desert cottontails and songbirds. Other places are Cabrillo National Monument (for tidepool life, shorebirds) near San Diego, Crystal Cove State Park (for shore and wading birds, especially in winter) near Laguna Beach, Upper Newport Bay Ecological Reserve (best late fall to early spring) near Newport Beach, Point Mugu State Park (sea lions, songbirds in spring) near Oxnard, Morro Bay and Montana de Oro state parks (sea mammals, marine and wading birds) near Morro Bay, Pismo Beach State Park (monarch butterflies, shorebirds and waterfowl in winter) near Pismo Beach, Point Lobos State Reserve (sea otters and harbor seals, magnificent scenery) near Carmel.

Midway along the California coast is another extremely important wildlife area: Monterey Bay. Just beyond the kelp beds of the bay is an abyss called Monterey Canyon which is deeper than Yosemite Valley not far to the east, or even than the Grand Canyon of the Colorado River. This submarine canyon supplies—fuels—one of the most diverse ocean environments along the entire North American Pacific Coast. Its nutrient-rich waters attract everything from microscopic plankton and clouds of silver anchovies to cormorants and sea otters and whales into the bay, often very close to shore. The Monterey Canyon, in fact, even influences the area's weather.

►

The once-common, then gravely endangered, California brown pelican is making a slow comeback. This one was photographed near Santa Barbara.

▼

Point Lobos State Reserve near Carmel.

Not all of these riches from the ocean are easy to see, and although this book is about nature rather than man, it is important to mention the fine Monterey Bay Aquarium that opened in 1984. It is the largest aquarium in America, and although constructed on the shell of an abandoned fish cannery, probably is the finest in the world. Best of all, it gives visitors an accurate, everchanging view of just what lives beneath the surface of Monterey Bay and how the organisms, from jellyfish to sharks, interact and conduct their daily lives.

For example, there is an entire forest of kelp growing in a single aquarium tank that holds 335,000 gallons of fresh sea water recycled every 79 minutes. The aquarium is 28 feet (or three stories) tall. A giant piston sends waves surging across the top of the tank to create the flow of sea water kelp needs to survive. Over 300 species of marine life live in this and 80 other natural environments, all easy to see and understand.

One afternoon after exploring the aquarium, we hiked westward along the jogging path of Ocean View Boulevard parallel to the rocky coast. The tidepooling can be good here, but this was high tide and we were soon distracted by a pair of sea otters swimming, grooming, and sometimes seemingly sleeping on the surface of the water. Other otters were within telephoto lens range just offshore. Our hike was postponed and we spent the rest of the

Sanderlings feeding along the surf line near Point Lobos.

▼

► A little green heron catches a frog in a lagoon near Santa Barbara.

▼ Sanderlings flush along the beach near Carmel.

▲

California or southern sea otters have made a fairly good comeback and can be seen near Monterey and Point Lobos.

afternoon following and photographing them. This may be the best place anywhere to watch wild sea otters. Not far distant, incidentally, in Monterey harbor, is an excellent place to see California sea lions close up.

The southern, or California, sea otter is a race of the species that once ranged the entire northern Pacific Rim, from Japan and the Aleutian Islands southward to Baja. American, Russian, British and Spanish hunters pursued the otters for their splendid fur until virtually all the animals were gone. The California population was reduced to fewer than 50 animals in 1911, when the species was first given legal protection. Now about 2,000, or less than one-tenth of its historic numbers, live along 220 miles of coastline from the Santa Maria River (Santa Barbara County) north to Año Nuevo Point in San Mateo County.

The most surprising thing about sea otters is their large size. Male adults may be five feet long and weigh from 70 to 90 pounds. A few individuals exceed 100 pounds. Females average four feet or so in length and weigh from 40 to 60 pounds. Their hind feet are webbed for swimming and diving. Short, stiff toes on the forefeet enable the animals to deftly handle food. On land a sea otter's locomotion is clumsy, and the animals can easily be caught by a man with a large net. But in the water, capture is another, entirely different matter.

A healthy sea otter's fur may be the finest, most luxurious (commercially speaking) in nature. It consists of very dense, fine underfur of inch-long fibers overlain by sparse guard hairs. The color varies from dark brown to nearly black, although very pale or silvery ones are sometimes found. Older animals often develop gray heads that, combined with their prominent whiskers, help explain an old sea otter nickname, "old man of the sea."

The seals and sea lions that share the sea otter's range depend on heavy layers of blubber to insulate them from the cold Pacific waters. But the otter survives by relying on air trapped in its dense fur to maintain body temperature. That explains why otters spend so much time grooming and rubbing their coats: if that fur ever becomes soiled or matted, as by an oil spill or ship's bilge discharge, the insulation is lost and the otter dies of hypothermia.

The daily search for food consumes a good bit of every otter's life. To obtain the 40 to 50 pounds of whole clams and other shellfish each otter requires each day, they can easily dive as deep as 250 feet. Peggy and I have seen them extract the meat of clams by cracking two together. More remarkable, they sometimes retrieve flat rocks which they place on their bellies as they float on their backs and then smash the shell of the clam against the rock.

A sea otter pops to the surface after a feeding dive.

California sea otters mate year around, so pups, weighing three or four pounds at ▼

▲

The appealing face of the California sea
otter helped save it from extinction.

►

A bull elephant seal scoops out a resting
place in sand after the breeding season.

birth, can be born at any time. Light brown in color, the pups are never left alone by their mothers except when they deep dive to forage. A few pups are then taken by bald eagles, sharks and killer whales, but human poachers and commercial fishermen who despise sea otters for the quantities of fish they consume are a much more significant factor in otter population losses. Left alone along California's beautiful shoreline, sea otters live from 15 to 20 years.

Just north of Monterey Bay, at the cool and windy Año Nuevo State Reserve near Pescadero, amid sand dunes, mudstone ridges and dark mounds built by polychaete worms, northern elephant seals come ashore early every December. It is the only mainland haulout of this species and is among the most important. The males engage in spectacular battles, the females give birth, breed, wean their young and moult, a process that lasts until April. Steller's and California sea lions engage in similar rituals on offshore Año Nuevo Island. All of this seal and sea lion activity has recently become popular enough to humans to qualify as an international wildlife attraction. In fact, the seal viewing is restricted to guided tours booked in advance, and these reservations must be made in November or earlier.

Even without the seal show, Año Nuevo is a most important sanctuary. We have seen loons, grebes, marbled murrelets and six of the seven species of gulls here. Green tree frogs are common, but we have never been able to find the San Francisco garter snakes or the Santa Cruz salamanders, both endangered, that are found here.

About 30 miles north of the San Francisco Bay area's six million people and traffic gridlock is an "island" separated from the rest of North America by the San Andreas Fault: Point Reyes National Seashore, where almost half of all the bird species in the United States may be seen. We have camped here often, once inadvertently and almost directly beneath the nest of an Anna's hummingbird that paid little attention to us or our orange tent. We have hiked many miles over established Point Reyes trails, although, unfortunately, too seldom in good weather. Still, we have met the uncommon tule elk and abundant black-tailed and fallow deer, plus other creatures, from snails and myotis bats (one of 13 species here) flying at dusk, to waterfowl and western flycatchers. Raccoons prowled around our tent at night, and from ocean cliffs we have looked down on the rocky haulouts of harbor seals and sea lions.

Sunshine can be elusive, at least it has been for us, at Point Reyes. Some years springtime seems to last from February, when the first wildflowers (poppies and irises) appear, until the marsh rosemary blooms toward the end of October. The golden days of autumn can last until Christmas, when the heaviest rains usually fall. The seashore also contains a 24,000-acre wilderness that runs from chaparral to steep cliffs overlooking the Pacific. Genuine wilderness along an ocean shore so near to so many people is a rare commodity on earth today.

Probably the strangest resident of this Point Reyes wilderness is the aplodontia, or mountain beaver, also caller a boomer, that is not a beaver at all. Instead, the aplodontia is a stocky, short-limbed rodent with small eyes, short ears and a stub of a tail. It chatters, whines and squeals when disturbed in the dense vegetation through which it wanders and tunnels. Its food is almost any green plant material, and it will eat bark. Boomers are not beloved by foresters because they climb into shrubs and saplings, and sometimes forest seedlings, eating off branches to form a ladder on their way to the top. We have been lucky enough to meet a number of mountain beavers while hiking during early, misty mornings.

The largest continental seabird nesting colony, about 300,000 birds of 12 species, nests on seven bleak islands of the Farallon NWR, 30 miles west of Point Reyes. About 7,000 seals annually breed here. The surrounding marine environment is considered so productive, yet so critical, that the area is closed to the public.

Anna's hummingbird on its nest at Point Reyes National Seashore.

▼

One memorable spring we drove northward from Point Reyes the short distance to the estuary where the Russian River flows into the sea. This area, officially designated

Sonoma State Beaches–Bodega Bay, attracts vast numbers of waterfowl and shorebirds and is a good destination for general birding. But we had come to photograph the hundred or so harbor seals that headquarter here during most of the year and that have become more tolerant of photographers than harbor seals have almost anywhere else.

Pacific green tree frog, photographed at Año Nuevo State Park.

We arrived on a morning when several dozen seals had hauled out on a sandspit formed by the river. Despite the vast open space available, most of the mammals were lying, as if dead, one on top of the next. We watched them for a time, cameras on tripods and ready for action that never happened. Eventually Peggy said, "I think they specialize and excel in sleeping." You look at the fat-as-Buddhas bodies, the large black eyes, either closed or slitted, and you notice that many seem to be smiling. It seems they are dreaming about seas full of fat, slow-moving fish, but the fact is that harbor seals must spend more time hauling out and resting than do other pinnipeds.

Despite their shape, harbor seals carry less blubber for their size than do their relatives. The fur on the harbor seals' handsome, dappled hides is less dense. Scientists have also learned that harbor seals carry less oxygen in their blood than their cousins, and their long periods of inactivity simply conserve needed energy. Harbor seals do almost all their foraging and feeding closer to shore than do other seals, which means they do not have as far to swim back to regular sleeping places—haulouts—in coves, harbors and such estuaries as the one at the mouth of the Russian River.

Sitting and watching the seals do nothing but occasionally roll over throughout the morning was fatiguing, and we were hungry and thirsty. So, we packed up our gear to begin the mile-long trek back to our van, parked beside Highway 101. That seemed to trigger some action. Several seals rolled over, and one female actually eased into the river's current. We sat down again to watch. Now, one by one, all the seals disappeared into the river. We figured they were headed to sea and, for the second time,

▲

Harbor seals feed on eels at the mouth of the Russian River.

we prepared to leave. A sandwich and a cup of coffee seemed like the best idea, but once more the activity of the seals changed our minds.

At first we could only see the backs of a few of the animals swimming erratically in shallow water close by. We could not tell what they were doing. Suddenly, an eel about two feet long squirted out of the water and onto dry land . . . with a seal lunging right behind it and finally catching it in its sharp teeth.

For the next half hour we had beachside seats to watch a feeding frenzy unlike any we had seen before. Apparently, a school of eels had moved into the river mouth to spawn, and the harbor seals were taking full advantage of it. We saw the seals violently shake their heads, eels twisting in their jaws. On at least two more occasions the eels tried desperately to escape the killers by launching themselves out of the water and onto the beach, where they landed, whipping from side to side, not five feet from

where we stood. It was a remarkable photo opportunity, but not an easy one. Trying to focus on some specific action was nearly impossible. It was well into the afternoon when the action finally slowed and then stopped, and most of our harbor seals were once again slumbering on the warm sand. When it was over we felt a familiar mixture of exhilaration and apprehension about the outcome of our shooting.

Several weeks later at home, then in Jackson Hole, Wyoming, we looked eagerly at our slides on a light table and found that the results were mixed. Most of the slides had been exposed a split second too soon or just too late to catch the peak of the action. Many of the images were out of focus, as we expected, but a few were clear and sharp enough to always remember that busy day we spent between Baja and Barrow.

▲

Harbor seals hauled out on the beach at the mouth of the Russian River.

Hawaii

Tern Island

daybreak is only a pale lemon glow in the east as Peggy and I grope in darkness toward a small storage building. Carrying armloads of photographic gear, we almost stumble over a pair of albatrosses with a large chick. They have bedded directly in our path. They honk and click their bills rapidly to warn us away.

"Not to worry," I say gently to the big birds, "we're friends."

Inside the shed we load our cameras, tripods and lenses into the wire baskets of two large, rusting tricycles left behind by military occupation forces years ago, and I pump air into the flattened tire of one of the bikes. Then we pedal out onto a bare, deserted landing strip that extends the length of eight or nine football fields and dead-ends in the Pacific Ocean.

The tricycle ride is a strange and surreal experience, especially in the dim, early morning light. Along the entire length of the airstrip we are accompanied by a Halloween symphony of moaning and croaking, braying and yodeling. There are birds on the ground and birds in the air. Some are landing, others are taking off. A few pass so close to us that we can feel the brush of their wings. One briefly lands on my baseball cap. Another catches a free ride atop a telephoto lens sitting in my tricycle basket.

By the time we reach the end of the runway, the sun is just clearing the horizon, washing hundreds of nesting seabirds in its golden glow. For the next two hours Peggy and I exchange not a single word. Instead we use the best of the warm photographic light to focus on red-footed boobies, nesting in heliotrope bushes, and male great frigatebirds inflating their scarlet throat pouches. We expose film with unabashed extravagance.

Midway Islands

Pearl and Hermes Atoll

Lisianski Island

Laysan Island

Gardner Pinnacles

Tern Island French La Perouse Pinnacle Frigate Shoals

Necker Island

Nihoa

Niihau

Kauai

Oahu HONOLULU

Molokai

Lanai

Kahoolawe Maui

Hawaii

▶

An endangered loggerhead turtle makes a beachhead on Tern Island.

▲

Endangered Hawaiian monk seal hauled out on Tern Island.

More than once, as soon as I find a bird in a perfect pose in my viewfinder, I am distracted, either by pairs of "dancing" albatrosses or by monk seals that lurch ashore expecting to spend the day sleeping exactly where I am standing. So, I gather up my equipment and move. Altogether, the morning is remarkable. No, *spectacular*. I have spent the last half-century photographing wildlife and wild habitats around the world and I can say with certainty that Tern Island is one of the most remote and vibrant wildlife areas left on Earth.

Tern is the largest of the small sand and coral islands that make up French Frigate Shoals, a lonely atoll near the center of the Pacific Ocean. A unit of the Hawaiian Islands, French Frigate Shoals is one of the northwestern island groups designated in 1909 by President Theodore Roosevelt as the Hawaiian Islands National Wildlife Refuge. Tern Island lies about 500 miles west of Honolulu. The nearest human settlement is on Kauai, 385 miles away. Midway Island, with a small military garrison, is 500 miles to the west. Beyond these spots, no people live permanently within 1,000 miles or so in any direction. Nor is Tern situated along any major ocean shipping lane, although its surrounding waters are all too familiar to commercial fishermen.

Nonetheless, Tern Island is a busy place. Every year, from April through June, as many as 400,000 seabirds of 15 species may be based (about half to nest) on Tern, which encompasses 37 acres of land, and nearby Whale Skate and East islands. Tern is also a sanctuary for the rare and endangered Hawaiian monk seal. In early 1991 this species' population was estimated at only 1,500. (The seals' Caribbean cousin has been considered extinct for 40 years, and probably fewer than 500 Mediterranean monk seals cling to existence in the Mediterranean and along the coast of Mauritania in Africa.) In addition, French Frigate Shoals is an important landfall for the endangered Pacific green turtle.

Our visit to Tern Island in April 1992 was not my first. In 1970 I joined the annual inspection trip, which was led by Gene Kridler, then the refuge's manager. We stopped at each of the islands in the chain: Nihoa, Necker, Lisianski, Laysan (which has the largest seabird population of all, and endemic species of duck and finch), Pearl and Hermes Atoll, and French Frigate Shoals. We camped for several days on Laysan but wasted little time on Tern because at that time there were few animals there. U.S. Coast Guard and other military forces had occupied the island off and on since 1943. After World War II, the Coast Guard built an elaborate station and barracks to house a permanent force of 25, but that base was relinquished in 1979 to the U.S. Fish and Wildlife Service. Since then Tern has been occupied mostly by a few biologists and wildlife researchers. Access is via a three-and-a-half-hour flight on small aircraft from Honolulu, or a long, sometimes rough, boat voyage. As a result of its isolation and minimal human intrusion, the seabirds have returned en masse to Tern Island.

Our 1992 trip to Tern was part of a regular resupply mission for the biological station's staff of four: acting refuge manager and Vermont native Jennifer Megyesi; her volunteer assistant, Rich Schauffler, who had studied Atlantic puffins in Maine and was investigating the island's red-tailed tropicbirds; marine mammalogist Mitch Craig of

Gray-backed terns.
▼

the National Marine Fisheries Service, who was keeping an eye on the monk seals (the French Frigate Shoals population of 800 has been undergoing a serious, mysterious decline); and virologist Doug Skilling of Oregon State University, who was assisting Craig and taking seal blood samples for analysis.

With a density of about 2,500 nesting pairs per acre on Tern Island, the birds would be nearly shoulder to shoulder if the various species did not utilize different habitats. We found them nesting like human apartment dwellers on four levels on, above, and below the same plot of ground. Some species—wedge-tailed shearwaters and Bonin petrels—nest in underground burrows they excavate as skillfully as do badgers and ground squirrels at home in Montana. Other birds—Laysan and black-footed albatrosses; sooty terns; masked boobies; spectacled, or gray-backed, terns; and brown, or common, noddies—nest on open ground. Red-tailed tropic birds and Christmas Island shearwaters also nest on the ground, but under vegetation.

Great frigatebirds, red-footed boobies and black noddies perch and construct their crude nests above the ground in the vegetation, either *Scaevola sericea* or *Tournefortia argentea*, the latter an excellent beach-binding plant. White, or fairy, terns build no nests at all but may balance their single

egg on a branch or rock. Fairy terns particularly seemed to like the ▲
window ledges and crannies of the old Coast Guard buildings. One
female fairy tern laid her egg and hatched the chick on the rusted
valve handle of an abandoned fuel tank.

A fairy tern hovers above as we photograph monk seals on the beach.

We know it is easy to spend too much time photographing male great
frigatebirds as they sit watchfully, wings outstretched and quivering, feathers flared
behind their red gular pouches, which they inflate like balloons during the breeding
season. Each time a female flies overhead, a hopeful male increases the fluttering of
his wings and waves his black, hooked bill in her direction. It is almost impossible
to stand anywhere on that lonely bit of real estate and not see red spots dotting the terrain.

The frigates' lifestyle is as interesting as their courtship posturing. They live by preying on—
mugging, really—their neighbors. Most of the time they attack boobies and terns in mid-air at sea,
causing them to drop their catch. The frigates then capture the fish before it hits the water. During
the nesting season, frigates scoop up unattended sooty or noddy tern chicks, too.

For sheer numbers, the black-and-white sooty terns predominate on the island, making up about
75 percent of the bird population. They occupy all the flat ground and even encroach on the airstrip.
The largest colony of masked boobies in the Hawaiian Islands nests and raises young among the
sooties. During our visit, the masked booby chicks were already heavier than their parents.

One morning, as a dark rain cloud covered the sun, I sat down beside the bare runway to eat a
candy bar and change film. Some distance away a masked booby with an all-white chick was preening
itself. Something, maybe the crinkling of the candy wrapper, brought the two boobies waddling
directly to my side. The adult pecked gently at my shirtsleeve and, owl-like, studied me until
departing, apparently unimpressed.

On another day we made the 30-minute run by boat across the lagoon to Whale Skate Island.

A male greater frigatebird displays to
attract a female.

▲

Greater frigatebird bachelors.

►

A mated pair of frigatebirds posed
unafraid for a portrait.

Unlike Tern, Whale Skate is bare, with only one *Tournefortia* shrub in the center, under which many masked boobies had gathered for shade. We also counted 24 monk seals and half that many green turtles basking on the coarse sand beach. As we anchored the boat at one end of the island, several turtles and seals came ashore on the opposite end.

Among the seals hauled out were three large females with pups. Biologists believe that one factor limiting Hawaiian monk seal numbers may be that mothers will abandon their pups if unduly disturbed by people. We kept a safe distance, and through long telephoto lenses watched and photographed one mother nursing her youngster. In time the female rolled over and brushed the baby away. Still hungry, the pup tried to nurse from a sea turtle that had just arrived in the gentle surf, and of course, was brushed away again. The pup then returned to its mother and fell asleep in the shade of her 500-pound body.

Probably no birds were more visible on Tern Island than the Laysan albatrosses, elsewhere called gooney birds—an appropriate description. Gooney birds do not nest until they are about seven years of age, and then pairs mate for life, often until they are 30 years old. We observed many chicks stoked with a daily diet of regurgitated seafood that were almost the same size as their parents. All day long the young albatrosses sat motionless under the hot sun like fat, brown-feathered Buddhas, their feet upturned for ventilation. Meanwhile, the adults were busy getting food for the chicks.

Takeoff is difficult for the heavy albatross at any time, but on windless days the effort required is great, and often comical. The albatrosses sought a long, open route on the runway, then ran full tilt into whatever breeze they could discern, large webbed feet pounding ever faster on the hard-packed surface. Huge wings flapping, they always managed to become airborne just before the watery end of the strip. Every return was a desperate, clumsy crash landing that sometimes bowled over unfortunate birds in the approach path.

Not all the Laysan albatrosses we observed had nested. Perhaps an equal number, not yet mature,

▲

Greater frigatebird on nest with chick.

▲

A young frigatebird tests its wings.

spent long hours practicing the species' courtship dances and rituals.

Even in this remote paradise, trouble may be brewing. Craig told us that within the past year the monk seal population may have dwindled by one-third, leaving only about 1,000 animals. As yet there are no clear explanations for the decline. With military presence almost gone from the northwestern Hawaiian Islands, human interference no longer seems a factor. Deteriorating water quality in the Pacific could be responsible, but more than likely the culprit is overfishing with modern long-lines and nets that drift for many miles. Fishing is banned within 50 miles of all the islands in the wildlife refuge, but the regulation is impossible to enforce with the small budget allotted to cover so vast an area. There is increasing evidence of illegal fishing activity.

Megyesi and Craig said that more of the plastic chemical light sticks used to illuminate Japanese fishing nets had washed ashore on Tern Island that year than had appeared in all previous years, and they had found Hawaiian monk seals on the beaches with fishhooks imbedded in their mouths. We photographed the desiccated skeletons of monk seals that had managed to drag themselves and their burdens to shore before dying there, entangled in heavy nets. Discarded fishing nets with dead sea creatures enmeshed in them regularly wash ashore on the island.

The night before we flew back to the high-rises of Honolulu I did not sleep soundly. Instead I listened, maybe for the last time, to the moaning of the shearwaters, the clicking of albatross bills and the haunting cries of other birds I could not clearly identify. I also recalled my first trip to this lonely archipelago; it began shortly after daybreak on a clear, calm morning in September 1970 when the U.S. Coast Guard cutter *Buttonwood* slowly cruised close to Lisianski Island and, on reaching a depth of ten fathoms, dropped anchor. An hour later, a 25-foot surf boat was lowered, loaded, cast away toward shore, and I began a remarkable adventure.

First let me explain that, like Tern Island, Lisianski was and is a virtually unknown 382-acre speck

of sand almost in the center of the Pacific Ocean. It is uninhabited and so remote that very few humans have ever set foot on its beaches. I remember going ashore, cautiously winding through a maze of coral reefs, and finally wading out onto hot sand.

An adult Hawaiian monk seal scans a beach before coming ashore.

The crew of the *Buttonwood* had dubbed us "the wildlife bunch," and later just "the wild bunch." Our group included wildlife biologists Gene Kridler and John Sincock, marine mammalogist Ken Norris (who had 20 years earlier discovered the first vaquita, or Gulf porpoise, in Baja California) and me. We carried assorted scientific and photographic equipment. What we found was a wildlife spectacle too few humans can ever enjoy.

Long before the surf boat touched on shore, clouds of noddy and sooty terns swarmed out to meet us. Boobies and great frigates with bat-shaped wings circled above the terns, and countless ruddy turnstones gathered at water's edge. Gray monk seals dozed and baked on the beaches in both directions from our landing. The din of the sea birds was so shrill and constant that it seemed we were wading in lukewarm water onto the beach of a strange planet.

"Back again," said Kridler, who was then one of the very few individuals to ever have previously landed on that lonely islet.

The distance around Lisianski is a mere three and a half miles, but over the powdery soft sand and in the brutal heat of autumn at 26 degrees north latitude, it soon seems more like 30 miles. Because this was an important working trip with limited time, Gene and John had to carry along enough gear to live-capture, hold, weigh and tag as many monk seals and green sea turtles as they

could catch. I was luckier—I had only to carry my cameras and a canteen of water which was too soon empty.

But what a remarkable hike it was. Altogether we counted 119 monk seals, which even then were considered endangered, and managed to tag most of the pups and yearlings.

The monks appear lethargic when on land, and most did not bother to move when we approached. Still, it is only practical and safe to tag only the smaller individuals because all have terrible teeth and resent being handled.

Monk seals are the oldest of all living pinnipeds, having existed anatomically unchanged for about 15 million years. The Hawaiian species evolved on this remote and isolated archipelago and probably never lived in any numbers on the main Hawaiian Islands. In fact, there is no word in the Hawaiian vocabulary for seal.

Monk seal pups are born from December through August, but most enter the world on sandy beaches in April or May. They can swim when only four days old. Adult females grow larger than do males, and a female's weight varies greatly during the year. A gravid female weighing 400 pounds might only weigh 300 pounds by the time her pup is old enough to fend for itself. Apparently, females fast during lactation and remain with their pups for that entire period, losing about two pounds for every pound gained by the pups. When she no longer is able to feed her youngster, the female heads out to sea to refuel. The pup must then suddenly survive on its own blubber.

Monk seal mating has rarely if ever been witnessed, but biologists have seen, from spring through fall, what appears to be monk seal courtship behavior. Females molt after the young are weaned. Of all seals, monks seem to suffer most from human disturbance, and many pups die from malnutrition when suckling is too often interrupted by people. Despite being the most tropical of seals, living on hot, sun-drenched shores, this species shows no special adaptations to its habitat. Its body temperature of about 98 degrees Fahrenheit is similar to that of other seals.

Besides the Lisianski monk seals, we also tagged four turtles we found basking on the beaches, the largest weighing 250 pounds, the smallest a four-pounder judged to be only one year old. We had

time for a cooling swim before the surf boat retrieved us and returned our party to the *Buttonwood* late in the afternoon. But our adventure had barely begun.

Lisianski is the farthest west (and just six degrees east of the International Date Line) of landfalls in the Hawaiian Islands NWR. The total land area of the refuge islands (otherwise known as the Leeward, Northwest, or simply the "bird islands") is only 1,800 acres, but the refuge also includes 250,000 acres of submerged reefs and shallow lagoons surrounding them. The only human habitation was on tiny Tern Island, which Peggy and I would visit later. The rest belonged exclusively to five million birds and includes some of the greatest sea bird nesting colonies on the globe. Many of the birds remain nearby the year around. It is an absolutely priceless wildlife sanctuary.

But there have been some problems in paradise. On certain islands in the past, guano diggers, plume hunters and the introduction of hares completely eliminated at least three native species: a flightless rail, a honeycreeper and a millerbird, while nearly dooming others.

Such inspection trips as ours on the *Buttonwood* were never pure pleasure because access to mid-ocean landfalls is almost always difficult. The refuge islands are remote from normal shipping lanes and landing on reefs or rocky shores anywhere in high seas is hazardous at best, and sometimes downright impossible. Only the U.S. Coast Guard has the means to regularly visit these islands and to put people safely ashore. Kridler depended upon their good cooperation.

From home I had flown to Honolulu and there transferred to a military charter flight to Midway, which is as well known for its nesting gooney birds—black-footed albatrosses—as for the crucial World War II sea battle. At Midway our "wild bunch" boarded the *Buttonwood*, which is really a buoy tender, and there began the sluggish (at 11 knots) voyage back eastward to Lisianski and beyond. From Lisianski it is an overnight run to Laysan where we would make a second beachhead, but this time also pitch a camp for a week's stay while the *Buttonwood* patrolled elsewhere.

Comparisons obviously are difficult, but Laysan may be among those places in the world most intensively utilized by birds. More than a million birds of 23 species use the 1,100 acres during any year for nesting and resting. That amounts to about 1,200 birds per acre. With this density, the birds must nest on "levels," as we found them on Tern Island. When approaching from the sea, the cloud of birds hovering overhead is visible long before Laysan's sand dunes, which are nowhere more than 40 feet above sea level.

Because of the protective surrounding barrier reefs, Laysan is a very easy island on which to land most of the time. By mid-morning all of our camping gear was deposited on the beach, and while we pitched a pair of tents on the nearest high dune, we watched the *Buttonwood* sail away. With that, all contact with civilization was severed, and for the first time ever I was marooned on a desert island. I say desert because our entire water supply had to be obtained from the Coast Guard cutter supply.

I have camped in more strange situations than I can remember, but none to match this one. Parent frigates fed their young on nests not far from our tent flaps, and young boobies soon discovered our tent's ridge poles to be perfect perches. Laysan finches, a rare species found nowhere else, ate bread crumbs from our outdoor table and at times practically from our hands. After dark, a wedgetail shearwater peered through the mosquito netting at the curious figures making notes inside, and then tried to dig a nesting burrow beneath the canvas floor. All night long the unearthly moaning chorus of wedgetail and Christmas Island

Red-footed boobies courting. The bird at left is sky-pointing.

▲

Red-tailed tropicbird chick on a nest
shaded by brush.

▲

Red-tailed tropicbird adult on nest
containing a single egg.

shearwaters and Bonin Island petrels rose and fell with the wind.

A week proved too little time to spend on Laysan. Most mornings I spent beside the lagoon in the center of the island. The lagoon's water is several times as salty as the surrounding sea. There I saw bristle-thighed curlews, wandering tattlers and turnstones, but I mostly spent the early hours trying to photograph the rarest waterfowl in the world at that time, the Laysan teal, which feeds primarily by skimming the water's surface for brine flies. Gene and John made several nighttime censuses (with spotlights) of the chocolate-colored teal and concluded that there were 150 on the island. That's a pitifully small world population, but once the number had been reduced to seven, and only a few years earlier the total living population was a precarious 30.

Gene and John tagged monk seals and turtles with complicated electronic transmitter equipment, and Ken Norris tried to record the underwater sounds that the seals use to communicate. One day we crossed the island to visit a derelict Japanese fishing boat that had run aground one stormy night in 1969. For a time it was feared that the vessel would bring European brown rats to the bird paradise, a potentially catastrophic event, but the ship, miraculously, had been clean.

Perhaps the most exciting time on Laysan was spent snorkeling over the living reefs that in places extend from far offshore right to water's edge. I had never before seen so many fishes of such incredible shapes and colors. A few I could identify were the wrasses, school blue ulua (a large member of the jack family), lionfish, angelfish, Moorish idols, parrotfish, tangs and several species of butterflyfish. Because we had encountered large schools of sharks when approaching Laysan aboard the *Buttonwood*, I kept a wary eye out for them. When the first one, probably a whitetip of about five feet, appeared one afternoon, I decided it was high time to swap snorkeling for bird photography and headed for the nearest beach.

During other visits to the refuge islands, Kridler and Sincock have made many sightings of

unusual or unexpected birds from as far away as Siberia and Alaska, and this trip was
no exception. On Laysan a single and curiously pale-colored, female pintail duck
accompanied a small flock of the endemic teal, and the first bird we encountered on
landing later at Tern Island was a mockingbird. But Tern was then an empty place
compared to what Peggy and I would find almost a quarter century later.

Nearly two days journey east of flat and sandy Laysan we came upon Gardner Pinnacles, the
remnant of an extinct volcano, the white-frosted black peak of which juts suddenly and straight out
of the sea. Only 40 acres in area and 280 feet high, it is the least important of the bird islands and
maybe that is just as well. Lashed constantly by breakers and washed by heavy swells, landing there is
seldom feasible, and twice in the past Gene had nearly lost his life in the attempt. On our trip the
ocean was extremely calm, but the landing was nevertheless a hairy business.

A rubber raft was used instead of the rigid surf boat. While a bosun's mate held the raft's nose
against a nearly sheer cliff, Gene waited until a swell lifted the boat as high as possible and then leaped
to a thin foothold while holding a rope. There he stayed until the others could jump and scramble up
the slick rock face.

French Frigate was our next stop, and then Pearl and Hermes Reef, which are important nesting
sites of green sea turtles. We lingered at Tern Island only long enough for the *Buttonwood* crew to go
ashore and enjoy the first cold beer in weeks at the soon-to-be-abandoned Coast Guard station. From
the tell-tale tracks we found on the beaches of nearby South and Whale Skate islands, we estimated
that about 48 turtles had recently come ashore to nest.

According to Kridler, from 900 to 1,000 green sea turtles nest on the French Frigate Shoals each year. Turtles Gene had personally tagged at the site have been picked up by commercial fishermen near Hilo, Hawaii, 600 miles distant.

Next to Gardner Pinnacles, 80-acre Necker Island is the most dangerous island on which to land. But as at Gardner the sea was comparatively calm and we landed without incident. The highest point (about 280 feet) on the island is reached by following a vertical crack in the face of a cliff. At the crest a climber is surprised to find the crumbling remains of a Polynesian temple abandoned some 700-800 years ago. Instead of the stone humanoid figures that earlier visitors had found here, we were greeted by roosting boobies and frigates that did not bother to fly from our approach. They only squawked at us or clapped their bills. We spent the day exploring a series of high ridges where we counted the first Bulwer's petrels, grayboked terns and blue-gray noddies of the trip. We had not noticed that while we were on the island the sea had grown heavier, and we had to jump for the raft between growing swells to return to the *Buttonwood*.

Nihoa is the last and easternmost of the Hawaiian refuge islands. Like Necker and Gardner it is a brooding and dark volcanic cone, but it is much larger, at 156 acres. On first approach it may appear that landing is totally impossible. The sheer cliffs that ring the island tower 800 feet above the

▲

Wedgetailed shearwater on its nest on Laysan Island.

A green sea turtle comes ashore to lay its eggs on Lisianski.

▼

Pacific and are deeply undercut. But by circling the island by boat it is soon apparent that there are two landing possibilities. One is a tiny beach, and the second a shelf of volcanic rock. From previous experience, Kridler selected the shelf, and we were only thoroughly soaked on reaching solid land.

Although Nihoa is an old Hawaiian word for bird, it is not a bird spectacle in the same sense as Laysan or Lisianski. Still, thousands of sooty and noddy terns, red-tailed tropic birds, frigates, petrels and boobies nest in most suitable sites. In addition, there is the endemic Nihoa finch, which is fairly abundant, and the endemic Nihoa millerbird, a species not discovered until 1923. Because it is shy and prefers to skulk in brush, it still is not an easy bird to see and, I found, nearly impossible to photograph. A rare loulu palm (*Pritchardia remota*) grows only on Nihoa, and only about 800 of the trees exist in two separate stands.

From Nihoa, our last stop, it was a day-and-a-half run back to Honolulu. As we pushed our way through the Kaulakahi Channel between Niihau and Kauai islands, it was evident that we had indeed left the bird islands far behind. No masses of birds wheeled and dived near the horizon, and none followed in the *Buttonwood's* wake as they had in the past. Nonetheless, at least for this member of the wild bunch, the trip had been an extraordinary wildlife adventure in the middle of the Pacific Ocean.

Greater frigatebirds return to land at sunset in the Hawaiian Islands NWR.

▼

Fort Stevens S.P. △
• ASTORIA

Ecola S.P. △
CANNON BEACH •

Three Arch Rock N.W.R. ▫ TILLAMOOK
•
Cape Lookout S.P. △

Yacquina Bay S.P. △

Cape Perpetua •YACHATS

Sea Lion Caves • FLORENCE
•
Oregon
Dunes
National
Recreation
Area

•
COOS BAY

BROOKINGS
•

Oregon

dURING OUR LAST TRIP THROUGH WESTERN OREGON, one species of its wildlife, a small creature that weighs about two pounds and is seldom seen, was prominently in the news. In fact, the northern spotted owl was a front page headline story from the California border northward to the Columbia River. "Bird Kills 1,000 Jobs," one newspaper headline announced. "Lumber Plant Will Fold," claimed another. "Who needs owls anyway?" was the title of an editorial in another Oregon daily. Most sentiment did not favor the furtive night hunter that had suddenly become a symbol for preserving the last old-growth forests in the state.

To tell the truth, the spotted owl was—and still is— a victim. For far too long we have been cutting down our magnificent Pacific Coast forests as fast as possible and with no thought to the future. Because the owl, which is an endangered species, needs old-growth forests in which to live, nest and survive, the birds were subjects of lawsuits (under the Endangered Species Act of 1972) designed to stop the rampant logging. But we should be saving what is left of our precious forests for their *own* sake, because they belong to all Americans, now and in the future, to see and enjoy.

As North American raptors go, the northern spotted owl is not an especially striking bird. Its range is restricted to coastal mountains from northern California to southwestern British Columbia. Lacking ear tufts, it resembles the more abundant barred owl, which is also brown with dark eyes that glow orange-red when in direct sunlight. But the underparts of the spotted owl feature fine horizontal markings, while those of the barred have a bold vertical pattern. The four- or five-note call, or hoot, most commonly heard has been translated as "Whooo are you, you all?"

Green sea anemones in tide pool at Cape Perpetua.

Biologists have carefully monitored Oregon's spotted owls and have analyzed the birds' requirements for survival. One need stands out above the rest: this bird must have mature forests that are more than 200 years old, with uneven-aged trees and multi-level canopies in which to forage, roost and nest. Almost never are they found in younger forests. About 1,000 acres of old-growth habitat is necessary to support one nesting pair. That habitat can be anywhere from near the ocean's edge to just below the subalpine forest zone. Their single most important prey is the northern flying squirrel, but they also catch plenty of wood rats, voles, deer mice and other rodents, as well as a few birds.

Spotted owls are known to spend the daylight hours roosting quietly in deep shade. Most are not especially shy of humans, so Peggy and I decided that we had to find one of these controversial birds for ourselves.

The state park system in Oregon is among the best in America. It is possible to travel U.S. 101, which parallels the Pacific Coast, and to pause at a different public campground every night for two weeks or so. From many of these campgrounds, excellent hiking trails lead onto ocean beaches as well as into forests where spotted owls live. Or should live.

Our plan was to travel the entire length of the Oregon coast, spending nights at the campgrounds, making long early morning and late afternoon hikes in search of the spotted owl. It is a plan we can recommend to anyone because it means seeing a remarkable number and variety of the state's other wildlife in its natural surroundings, as we did.

Near Yachats, at Cape Perpetua (which is a U.S. Forest Service rather than an Oregon state area), a thickly forested headland that rises sharply more than 800 feet above the Pacific surf, our hikes produced everything from dark-eyed juncos, rufous-sided towhees and rufous hummingbirds to chipmunks and black-tailed deer. At night we heard the haunting call of a great horned owl not far beyond the campground's perimeter. We hiked downward to tidepools alive with sea stars, sea urchins, hermit crabs and anemones. Offshore, rhinoceros auklets and marbled murrelets rode the blue waves. But no spotted owl here.

Yaquina Head, near Newport, was another natural area where we probably should have

▼
The western toad lives, but is declining, in old Oregon forests.

▲
The tufted puffin is a nester in and on offshore rocks and stacks.

◀
Rhinosceros auklet is a seabird you might see walking anywhere on Oregon's beaches.

Pigeon guillemots at Sea Lion Cave.

Jellyfish drifting offshore.

Pelagic cormorants near Yaquina.

lingered to wait for lower tides, to explore the tidepools. Offshore here we counted pigeon guillemots, tufted puffins, cormorants and common murres. Several puffins preened in the turbulent water close to shore and to us. We did not see any of the gray whales passing the Head, as had the visitors two days before. The whales often swim very close to land here during migration and are surprisingly easy to see. But no spotted owls hereabouts, either.

Some other excellent areas where we camped and explored were Fort Stevens State Park (near Astoria), Ecola State Park (near Cannon Beach, where there usually are many tufted puffins on and around Haystack Rock), Cape Meares State Park and Three Arch Rocks NWR (near Tillamook). There were many sea and shorebirds—most notably pelagic cormorants, guillemots and western gulls—at Cape Lookout State Park and Letart Bay. We arranged our schedule to be at Dean Creek, a woodland-wetland-meadow mosaic along the Umpqua River not far from Reedsport, at daybreak, to see the herd of Roosevelt elk that roam here. But on

this day our timing was not the best. A dense fog rolled in from the sea and transformed the scene into something like dim, gray, out-of-focus photographs. But out in the murk Peggy spied a dark V-shaped movement. Viewed through binoculars, the movement became ears of an elk. The more we looked, the more elk ears we saw appearing and disappearing in the fog and dense vegetation. Before our viewing was totally obscured and rain began to fall, we had also seen the velvet antlers of a young elk bull.

▲

Sea Lion Cave is one of the largest sea grottos in the world. Sealions shelter here, especially in winter.

Frequent fog is unavoidable by anyone wandering along the Oregon coast for very long. It also can be a blessing. Simply a cloud that clings to the ground, fog is created by a collision of warm, moist air with much cooler air. The phenomenon helps to keep the coastal strip the coolest part of Oregon every summer. It also makes the coast the warmest area of the state in winter. Strange as it may seem, late spring and early fall are normally the warmest, driest seasons.

One afternoon we turned off U.S. 101 midway between Newport and Florence and found a secluded campsite in the Carl G. Washburne Memorial State Park. This is not among the best known of the coastal parks but it is a splendid base for hiking the trails inland into the area's tall evergreen forests, which are dominated by Douglas firs. Late in the afternoon we put cameras and binoculars

into rucksacks and started walking, eyes and ears open. Not far beyond the
campground I caught sight of a large bird—an owl—gliding down and away from a
tree perch, moving directly away from us. "Spotted," I said hopefully to Peggy.

Following the flight path of the owl, we carefully watched ahead and above us.
No wind blew, and the forest was absolutely quiet. In a few minutes we found our bird,
and this time it sat motionless, watching us with large, round eyes while we focused
our binoculars on it. But disappointment: the spotted turned out to be a young great
horned owl. Later we found another owl, this one a western screech. That night, under
canvas, we again heard the hooting of great horned owls, a sound familiar around many Oregon
campgrounds. At daybreak we were awakened by red squirrels chattering just outside our tent. But the
morning hike, pleasant and invigorating as all the rest, revealed no spotted owl.

Because Oregon's coast has been spared so much of the rampant development that has claimed
seashores elsewhere, there are a still diverse and healthy wildlife populations from top to bottom. You
might possibly (although not very easily) find all of the 96 mammal species (65 on the land, 31 in the
sea) that either live year around or migrate past in the ocean. The Roosevelt elk is the largest of the
land mammals; it can be seen at the Jewell Meadows Wildlife Area near Astoria as well as where fog
frustrated us at Dean Creek.

We have seen a good many Columbian black-tailed deer when hiking and driving through coastal Oregon. However, of all North American deer, they are usually the most furtive, and they are very difficult to observe in the dense habitat they prefer to inhabit most of the year.

There are two periods when the odds of encountering a blacktail are greatly improved, however. The first is in June when an eagle-eyed hiker in a forest might come upon a white-spotted, reddish fawn hiding motionless and well camouflaged as its mother browses out of sight, but always nearby. The other period is when a blacktail's guard is down, especially a buck's, during fall when ripe fruit has fallen to the ground in abandoned orchards. This annual bounty takes much of the deer's attention. Fall also marks the onset of the rut, when male deer lose much of their normal caution in their search for does ready to breed, and a buck may stop to look briefly back at a hiker before bounding off.

Depending upon with whom you meet and discuss the matter, black bears, cougars (or mountain lions) and bobcats are either very numerous—"too numerous for anybody's good"—or absent altogether in Oregon. The truth is that, although seldom encountered, all three do survive here in at least fair numbers. That is also true of beavers and red and gray foxes, but not of America's cleverest carnivore, the coyote. These wild dogs are seen

We found these barn owl young in an ancient dead tree nest, not in a barn.

▼

A strong surf pounds the coast where many harbor seals live.

Sea otters may occasionally be seen along Oregon's coast.

▼

Rufous hummingbirds spend summers in Oregon and migrate to Latin America for the winter.

with increasing frequency, however, particularly around some beaches and campgrounds, and on shrubby headlands and scattered, open pasture lands.

Next to a sighting of an endangered snowy plover, our most indelible memory of the Oregon Dunes National Recreation Area was a morning along the Bluebill Lake Trail when we sighted a pair of coyotes hunting in meadows saturated with dew. They captured several mice, or other very small creatures we could not identify, by leaping into the air and then arching downward, apparently connecting precisely with their prey on the ground.

This National Dunes area, with 40 miles of ocean shore and diverse habitats ranging from coastal forest to salt marshes and estuaries, is a remarkable place anytime, but for us it is especially so in fall and winter. Then the vacationers have returned home and we have the wildlife of Oregon nearly to ourselves; in fact, about 400 different species are on hand much or most of the time. The tundra swans at South Jetty are winter migrants from Alaska, but it is easy to be distracted by the loons and grebes and other migrants as well as by foraging raccoons or a wandering striped skunk. Harbor seals and California and Steller's sea lions are found at Oregon Dunes. This may be the extreme northernmost limit of the California sea lion's range as well as the southern limit for Steller's sea lions. Despite the common "sea lion" nomenclature, there is a good bit of difference between the two marine mammals, beyond their north-south separation of ranges.

California sea lions are the familiar "trained seals" you meet in zoos and circuses. They are shore-living mammals seldom found farther than ten miles out to sea. Steller's sea lions are the largest of all sea lions. Adult males measure about nine feet long, from nose to tip of tail, and weigh a half ton or more. Cows measure six or seven feet and average about 600 pounds in weight. (Contrast that to the California bulls at 600-700 pounds and females at 200-250 pounds.) Newborn Stellar's sea lion pups, usually born in June, weigh between 40 and 45 pounds.

Steller's sea lions, probably numbering in the millions, originally ranged northward from northern California to Alaska and then westward along the Aleutian chain to Kamchatka and the Arctic islands of eastern Asia. A summer haulout on Marmot Island (east of Afognak Island in the Gulf of Alaska) once contained 15,000 animals. When Peggy and I visited there with Seal Bay guide Roy Randall in 1980, Marmot was believed to hold the largest concentration of the species anywhere. Today, as almost everywhere else, only a fraction of that number haul out on Marmot. In some areas these sea lions have vanished altogether and are now classified as a threatened species.

In spring, Oregon paintbrush is widespread.

At least in one place in Oregon, Steller's sea lion numbers have not drastically ▼

▲

Raccoons are common mammals in the coastal strip.

◄

Black bears live near many Oregon beaches, but are not often seen.

►

The controversial spotted owl we finally found in Portland.

fallen. Oregon Cave, one of the world's largest sea caves, is a vast, multi-colored cavern that opens onto the Pacific Ocean along U.S. 101 between Newport and Florence. It is a commercial attraction (with an admission charge) at which visitors use an elevator to descend deep into a rocky headland to a unique viewpoint which looks into a grotto as wide as a football field and as deep as a 12-story building. Lichens, algae and minerals stain the grotto walls with many colors. Through fall and winter, especially during stormy weather, 150 to 200 Steller's sea lions haul out on rock piles inside the cave. In spring and summer, only a few Steller's use the cave, but they are easily visible on nearby rocky islands just offshore. It is interesting to note that every winter a few male California sea lions migrate northward from California to spend the cold months in and around the caves. In springtime, nesting pigeon guillemots, pelagic cormorants and rhinoceros auklets can almost always be seen here, too. It is a spectacular place to visit.

Despite making plenty of footprints in likely places from California to the Columbia River, we did not find our spotted owl until the very end of our last Oregon trip. We finally caught up to the elusive and embattled bird at the Washington Park Zoo, west of Portland, where technicians were rehabilitating one that had been injured. It was recovering and would soon fly away. We hope that spotted owls will always be out there, wild and free, in lush old-growth forests that we were wise enough to preserve for all time.

Washington

For more than a year, a sea lion bull, nicknamed "Herschel" by news writers, stole plenty of newsprint from the spotted owl, especially around Seattle and other parts of western Washington. Weighing in at about 800 or 900 pounds, Herschel was blamed for devastating an entire run of steelhead trout, a very popular game species among anglers.

The story began when the animal appeared at the entrance to the Lake Washington Ship Canal, a bottleneck through which the migrating steelhead must pass to eventually reach their spawning grounds in Cedar Creek and its tributaries. These trout spend most of their lives in the ocean, returning to such freshwater streams as the Cedar only to spawn. Unlike salmon that die after spawning, steelhead return to the sea every year. A single fish may make several round trips during its lifetime.

◄◄

Black-tailed deer at Hurricane Ridge in Olympic National Park.

Vancouver Island

Strait of Juan de Fuca

Ozette Lake

PORT ANGELES

LA PUSH

Bogachiel R.

Hoh River

OLYMPIC NATIONAL PARK

Olympic National Park

Queets R.

Puget Sound

SEATTLE

Lake Quinault

Gray's Harbor

Willapa Bay

Columbia R.

From May through November, Herschel and three or four smaller sea lions, probably females, would lurk just below the fish ladder at Seattle's Ballard Locks, the steelhead's only passage between Puget Sound (the Pacific Ocean) and Lake Washington, where fisheries workers could watch them. Once these agents saw Herschel and his friends capture 13 steelhead in just an hour and a half. No wonder that in 1985 about 1,500 fewer fish than anticipated reached the Cedar River spawning riffles. The annual spawning run had been reduced by about 80 percent.

Inevitably, these sea lions became a tourist attraction. Each weekend, crowds appeared to watch the action, which sometimes was exciting. But fishermen didn't think it was so funny when their sport dwindled down to almost nothing. Nor could state and federal fisheries biologists do more than try to frighten the sea lions away with firecrackers and ultrasonic devices. But these noisemakers worked for only a short time, until Herschel became used to them. It was almost as if the huge sea lion knew that he was protected by the 1972 Marine Mammals Act. Herschel was simply living in the wild on a natural food source. Eventually, he disappeared. No one knows where or why.

Hurricane Ridge in Olympic National Park is home to deer, black bears, marmots, and goats.

▼

The entire coastline of Washington, including the shores of Puget Sound, is a very

good wildlife area, not unlike those we have described in Oregon, and includes many of the same animal residents. The tidal flats, bays and inlets support an exceedingly rich shellfish, or bivalve, resource. Olympia and Pacific oysters, razor and butter clams, geoducks, cockles and northern abalone are a few of the most abundant. Speaking of abundance, a single female Pacific oyster (a species introduced from Japan in 1902) can produce up to 200 million eggs in a season, expelling them into the water where they are fertilized by the males. Only a few of the eggs survive, but the rest help feed a great variety of other edge-of-the-sea creatures that are near the bottom of the food chain.

Nowhere in North America, south of Alaska, is the meeting of sea and land more beautiful than the wild 57 miles of Washington coastline preserved as part of Olympic National Park. Walk the two-mile roadless section of this shore between the surf and fern-carpeted rainforests and you pass tidepools teeming with life, many seabirds, rock pinnacles, and strange sea stacks offshore. Altogether this might be the ultimate, solitary beachcomber's paradise. But water's edge is only the beginning— the bottom—of a national park full of wildlife from sea level to the snow-capped crest of Mt. Olympus, at 8,010 feet. One German naturalist who had spent the entire summer of 1993 trekking in the Olympic Mountains wrote in the national park guest book that, "I have seen more wildlife wonders here in August than in wandering all of Europe all my life."

The 900,000-acre Olympic National Park, a wilderness that occupies most of the Olympic Peninsula, is almost entirely surrounded by the sea: the open Pacific Ocean on the west, the Strait of Juan de Fuca on the north, Puget Sound to the east. If clouds and rain do not hang too low over the mountains, salt water is visible from many of the highest peaks and ridges. Peggy and I began our exploration of the Olympics when we drove   ▼

California gull forages on the Washington shore.

southward and upward from our campground at Heart of the Hills toward Hurricane Ridge, where the auto road ends and good hiking trails begin. What we found that sunny summer morning were calendar scenes of Columbian black-tailed deer grazing in purple lupine. Most of these deer were does with month-old fawns that paid little attention to us. A few bucks with antlers in the velvet were more shy.

Although it was a splendid and invigorating morning for hiking, we spent much of it sitting and just watching, soaking up golden sunshine. Besides the numerous deer, we studied the Olympic marmots, a drab-brown subspecies of marmots (or rock chucks), grazing on the only place they exist in the world: the high grassy slopes of the Olympics. Occasionally one sentinel marmot would stop suddenly, sit erect and watch us for a few seconds to reconfirm that we were not a danger. But then suddenly all vanished into their underground dens, where they stayed until long after a small black bear had passed out of sight on the mountainside far below us.

Another morning, this one cool and cloudy rather than sunny, we parked at a trailhead half way between Olympic Park headquarters and Hurricane Ridge. From there we began slowly climbing the steep switchback trail that can only be described as a lung-buster. At the top, on Klahhane Ridge, we hoped to find the mountain goats that preferred that lofty environment. Especially with all the camera and foul weather gear, lunch and water in our backpacks, plus an intermittent light rain, it was not a

pleasant climb, and on one nearly vertical pitch we almost turned back. But near the summit we met a nanny, followed by a kid, walking downhill toward us. They were followed by a second female with twins. All five passed us with hardly a glance in our direction before disappearing into stunted evergreens.

The Olympic marmot on Hurricane Ridge.

▲

Mountain goats are handsome but unwelcome residents of Klahhane and other high ridges in Olympic Park.

Nor did the four male mountain goats we found at Klahhane's summit seem greatly surprised by our arrival. Two of these were bedded close together at the edge of a precipice where Klahhane Ridge fell away to gray, misty eternity. One misstep here and it would be the last one. The other two billies nibbled at the sparse vegetation that still grew from cracks in the rocks in that stark, lonely place. We photographed all of them against cloud backgrounds until a light drizzle gradually became a determined downpour. The goats did not mind the weather, but we did, and began a long retreat down the steep, slippery trail.

For several years now those mountain goats we photographed on Klahhane and elsewhere in Olympic Park have worn out their welcome. As I write, an estimated 1,200 goats roam freely (or infest, according to Park Service biologists) the lonely high ridges. Since our rainy day hike, there have been a number of programs to reduce goat numbers, with the goal of eliminating them entirely, and probably with good reason.

The mountain goat is a goat-antelope, related only to the chamois of Europe, rather than a true goat. It is native to the Cascade Mountains of Washington and to other coastal ranges of northwestern North America. But like others of the "missing eleven"—the grizzly bear, wolverine, red fox, lynx, mountain sheep, porcupine, golden-mantled ground squirrel, pika, water vole and bog lemming—goats are not natives of the Olympic Mountains. During the Pleistocene ice age, an advancing glacier from Canada cut off the Olympic Peninsula from the rest of Washington and left only some peaks poking above the ice. Somehow, never in the intervening 14 million years since the glaciers vanished, did the missing 11 endemic Washington species ever manage to cross the 75 miles of lowland forest between the Cascades and the Olympics to reach what is today Olympic National Park.

During the 1920s, prior to the Olympic Mountains receiving national park status, a dozen or so goats were introduced there from Alaska and Canada. Since then the animals have flourished, virtually predator free, and have been extremely destructive of the area's unique, fragile vegetation. Their habits

Olympic mountain goat kids playing on a lingering snowbank.

of trampling and wallowing, for which they excavate large areas of soil to find relief from heat and insects, have eroded shallow alpine soils and have endangered many sensitive alpine plants. Today, 40 plant species of the Olympics are regarded as endangered, threatened or sensitive. Ten of these are rare endemics found only on this peninsula. Now the goats may not have much more time to graze in Olympic National Park, where they are officially regarded as an exotic species.

At intervals from Olympic Park northward to Glacier Bay in Alaska, goats live within sight of the Pacific Ocean. Viewed anywhere at any time, they are impressive, agile and powerful animals that are able to survive in steeper, more precipitous terrain than any other large mammal.

Giving the goat its characteristic forward-leaning profile are coarse guard hairs—which may grow eight inches long by late autumn—along its back and down its front legs. The animal's long chin whiskers are partly responsible for its "goat" designation. The mountain goat's dense underfur is very fine, compares favorably with fine cashmere, and enables it to withstand bitterly cold and damp winters.

It often seems that mountain goats were programmed by Nature to butt one another at any opportunity. We have seen nannies butt other females, even when they meet on a thin cliff ledge. Kids begin to butt one another from the day they are old enough to stand on four feet, which is almost immediately after birth. A nanny will usually butt any kid that is not her own and that stands in her path. The most vigorous butting of all takes place in the breeding season, from late October until December, when the males square off.

Naturalists who have studied goats report that most rutting clashes between males do not end in serious injury. Occasionally, however, there are fatalities when a billy is butted over a precipice or is too deeply punctured by the short, black, pointed horns of another male. In Alaska, I once saw a large billy butt a smaller one off a sloping ledge. The smaller goat fell about 12 feet into a jumble of jagged

rocks where it should have been critically injured or killed. However, after a moment or two, the animal stood up and climbed back onto the same ledge.

On other occasions we have watched mountain goat kids only a few weeks old cavorting crazily, butting and jumping over one another near the edges of lingering Olympic snowfields. These youngsters seem to develop physically much faster than most other wild young. Time and again we have seen precocious kids try to butt their playmates off steep places into oblivion, which may partially explain why the first-year-survival rates of kids is only about 50 percent.

Another large mammal is making a last stand in Washington. Taxonomists generally recognize 30 different subspecies of white-tailed deer living in North America. One of these, the Columbian whitetail, once ranged along the Pacific coast of Oregon and Washington where it was rather isolated from all other subspecies. No one really knows exactly how widespread and numerous the Columbian whitetails were. The explorers Lewis and Clark reported them abundant along the Columbia River in 1806, but by about 1968 (when the U.S. Department of the Interior officially classified them as an endangered species) they were almost extinct, largely victims of land clearing for agriculture.

▲
The Columbian whitetail, an isolated, now rare subspecies, survives in one national wildlife refuge and a few nearby woods.

◄
The western screech owl lives in cool evergreen forests.

Individual deer normally lived their entire lives on small home ranges and could not tolerate the radical change in their environment.

Now, in the 1990s, several hundred Columbian whitetails survive on the relatively small (5,200 acres) Columbian White-tailed Deer National Wildlife Refuge on the lower Columbia River. About half of the sanctuary is on the river's north bank between Skamokawa and Cathlamet; the balance is on adjacent Tenasillake Island. The deer are fairly easy to see, especially in fall and winter, from the refuge road that encircles the mainland portion. In winter the whitetails are joined here by Roosevelt elk that migrate down into the river bottoms from the uplands.

The Roosevelt, or Olympic, elk is the heaviest of the five surviving subspecies of elk (one subspecies is extinct). Its original range in the United States was very nearly the same as that of the Columbian whitetail but also included Vancouver Island, British Columbia.

Although Olympic National Park is far better known for its problem goats, it is the best place we have found to see Roosevelt elk, the world's second largest member of the deer family (after moose). Roosevelt elk bulls stand five feet at the shoulder and weigh from 700 to about 900 pounds. Cows (females) are smaller. By motoring the park's roads or, better, hiking the damp trails, you might meet Roosevelt elk anywhere. In summer, the elk usually migrate from subalpine heights, which they share with marmots, Douglas squirrels and black bears, to ocean shores in late fall, where shearwaters skim the waves in the background. Particularly good places to watch elk are in the Hoh, Bogachiel, Elwha and Queets River valleys, where herds of the hungry animals keep a park-like trim on meadows at the edges of the dense rainforest. As many as a hundred might appear together in one place. From these same meadows every fall comes the haunting, calliope bugling of elk bulls and the crash of their antlers during the rut. These are primeval sounds and sights worth traveling far to see.

▲

The Roosevelt elk, the largest race of American elk, thrives on the Olympic Peninsula.

►

A Roosevelt, or Olympic, elk harem during rutting season.

British Columbia

As a bald eagle flies, Chilko Lake is just east of British Columbia's southwestern coastal mountains and not far from numerous inlets of the Strait of Georgia. But to reach Chilko's outlet, where the Chilko River originates, sockeye salmon must travel about 450 miles from the sea to spawn every summer. They enter the Fraser River from saltwater (where they have lived for three years) near Vancouver, swim eastward, then north, next west and finally south in an almost circular route into the Chilko. Here and in many smaller tributaries, between September 15th and 25th, the shallow riffles glow red with the bodies of sockeyes, from 500,000 to a million of them. Like so many of the wildlife spectacles of North America's Pacific Coast, it is an extraordinary sight to see, especially if you can slip into hip boots and wade out into the center of it.

A generation or so ago it was possible to see such salmon spawning sights in many headwaters of Oregon and Washington, but the deadly combination of logging, dams, livestock overgrazing and contamination by introduced hatchery fish have all but wiped out such centuries-old spawning runs in the United States. This may also happen soon in British Columbia, where a low standard of timber harvest has been in progress for decades. As I write (1994), Chilko is among the last and southernmost grand-scale salmon runs surviving in the world.

Naikoon Prov. Park

PRINCE RUPERT

KITIMAT

Queen Charlotte Islands

Banks Island

Queen Charlotte Strait

Cape Scott Prov. Park

Chilko Lake

Vancouver Island

Strathcona P.P.

Strait of Georgia

VANCOUVER

PORT ALBERNI

Pacific Rim N.P.

VICTORIA

▲

Sockeye or red salmon swim upstream
to spawn.

Walk out slowly into the cold current during the peak of the run and stand motionless for a while. When I did this, the torpedo-shaped, scarlet fish milled all around me in schools and singles. Those with grotesquely hooked jaws, huge teeth and humped backs I recognized as males. Some bumped into my ankles. Some lurched clear out of the water and circled, searching for ripe females in this ancient ritual of breeding that ends in death.

It is well known that all five species of Pacific salmon—king (or chinook or tyee), silver (or coho), chum (or dog), pink (or humpback) and sockeye (or red)—begin life in clear, freshwater streams. Young hatch from eggs dropped and fertilized in gravel streambeds, and in spring they migrate down to the sea, where they grow to maturity in from two to five years. The adults then find their way back into the same waterways of their birth and spawn at the same time of year as their parents did. Soon after spawning, all Pacific salmon die and decompose. Death and renewal.

The abdomen of each of the sockeye females that surged all around me bulged with thousands of eggs. The males pursued the "hens" and fought off other males. When all had entered the Fraser

River weeks before to begin the long migration, they were bright silver in color. That metallic sheen quickly faded to rose, and then brightened to the red of the spawning fish. I saw some beginning their last color change, the scarlet beginning to fade to a dull gray. A few, spawned out, drifted helplessly, dying. Bald eagles, a wolverine and a number of black bears appeared on the scene. The bears were the busiest, gorging on the salmon carcasses to store fat and energy for the long winter of hibernation ahead. For a few brief days, living, for the scavengers, would never be easier.

Like most of the Baja to Barrow coastline, that portion belonging to British Columbia is simply stunning. From just north of Vancouver to Prince Rupert and the Alaska border, much of it remains evergreen and pristine, at least when viewed from the water. Such a viewpoint is easily possible because the Alaska Marine Highway, or marine ferry, travels the entire length of the province, from the port of Bellingham, Washington, northward. These efficient car ferries cruise in calm waters sheltered from the open ocean by the hundreds of islands that lie off the mainland shore. One summer, Peggy and I drove and hiked and camped the length of Vancouver Island, the largest of these barrier islands. We began by boarding the busy ferry at Port Angeles on Washington's Olympic Peninsula and disembarking at Victoria, British Columbia. We then continued northward to Pacific Rim National Park, a narrow, natural sanctuary on the west coast.

▲

A male sockeye salmon shows its characteristic hooked jaw and large teeth.

▲

Sockeyes enter fresh water from the sea silvery in color and gradually change to scarlet.

Most of Pacific Rim is a virgin forest of tall red cedar, hemlock, spruce and fir trees that tower over an almost impenetrable undergrowth of ferns and shrubs, here and there accessible by good walking trails. Even in high summer the park was cool with almost daily fogs and rain. We did not find many birds or mammals in that moist environment, but this might be the best of all the continent's wild beaches on which to explore tidepools, rocky headlands and ocean caves where limpets, mussels and barnacles cling to rocks despite the relentless pounding of thunderous waves. One morning we also watched a small flock of drake harlequin ducks easily riding a treacherous surf.

▲

The northern pygmy owl hunts in Pacific coastal forests.

◀

A caterwauling cougar on Vancouver Island.

►

A small pond in Pacific Rim National Park.

There is a very sad aspect to Pacific Rim that no visitor can ignore. All of the old-growth forests for miles around the park and right up to the park's boundaries have been logged. No bit of vegetation taller than a man's knee has been left. Not many months before our British Columbia venture, we had explored Brazil's besieged (by loggers) Amazon rain forest to see the destruction so widely trumpeted in the world's press. Compared to the devastated Canadian forests, the Amazon's seemed more like a vast conservation area. Another factor to be considered is that the terrain in British Columbia is mountainous and prone to terrible erosion from the frequent downpours that occur here. The Amazon Basin is flat.

From Pacific Rim we continued through Port Alberni, where hundreds of environmentalists from all across Canada had gathered together to protest further destruction of one of the largest tracts of ancient temperate rainforests remaining on earth, at nearby Clayoquot Sound. Drenched by ten feet of rain each year, trees as tall as 25-story buildings, 15 feet in diameter and estimated to be 1,500 years old, stand here in a seemingly Jurassic-like forest that looks as it did 5,000 years ago. We became acquainted with some of these protestors and saw some arrested for their activities. As I write, the status of the charges against them is still officially undecided. But greed and quick profits usually prevail in spite of the consequences.

Even serious problems can be forgotten in places such as Strathcona Provincial Park, a mountainous 500,000-acre wilderness "island" in the middle of both the destruction and of Vancouver Island. Hiking the park trails past wildflower gardens and through fragrant red cedar forests, we encountered black-tailed deer and elk, even a not-so-shy wolverine. One of these trails led to Della Falls, the highest waterfall in Canada, which plunges almost 1,500 feet in three cascades.

We hurried from Strathcona northwestward, through more depressing clear cuts, toward a tiny community, Telegraph Cove, which has recently been in the conservation news headlines. Located on narrow Johnstone Strait, the cove is suddenly known as the best destination anywhere for anyone who wants to see orcas, or killer whales, sometimes lots of them, at close range.

◀

Wolverines are not easily seen, but do appear regularly along salmon spawning streams.

▼

The cougar lurks on Vancouver Island, but is a predator that is rarely seen.

There are really two kinds of killer whales: those of fact and those of fiction. At times the two are very similar. Both are fast and fearless hunter-killers. An Alaskan native carver of totem poles and miniature orcas once confided to me that killer whales ranked above God. The killer whale of fiction is the one that stalks men stranded on ice floes or in small boats, deliberately overturning them for a good hot meal, and that rip apart commercial fishermen's nets just for the sport of it. Both of these old perceptions have been widely accepted for a long time.

Scientifically, orcas are among the largest of the toothed whales, a classification that includes the dolphins and porpoises. (The other cetacean classification contains the much larger whale-bone whales, such as blues, grays and humpbacks, which filter feed on plankton.) Full-grown killers average 20 feet long, but some dominant males might reach 30 feet, weigh eight tons and have six- or seven-foot-high dorsal fins. Of all sea creatures, orcas may be the best known and easily recognized by their sleek, streamlined shapes, black above and white below (with a white patch above and behind each

►

The black bear is another animal that takes advantage of salmon concentrated on such spawning streams as the Chilko.

▼

Canada lynx is another predator of British Columbia forests.

eye), and because of the numerous captive killer whales performing in marine shows and aquaria.

Next to man, these may be the longest-lived of all mammals. They may also be the most intelligent, argue some biologists, pointing out how well the whales have responded to training for exhibition. Orcas have been sighted in all the world's oceans, but are most commonly met today in Antarctica and especially in the eastern Pacific. They prefer water between freezing and 50 to 55 degrees Fahrenheit. Being mammals, they must breathe air, but they can spend as long as 30 minutes underwater between breaths.

Single killer whales are very seldom sighted; they usually travel in family groups or packs, called pods, of a dozen or more animals. Pods are known to temporarily join other pods to form larger living, hunting and breeding units. As carnivores go they are very efficient, moving over the ocean in almost military style, with a "point" whale well in front and "flankers" spread out on each side.

Orcas make two kinds of sounds. One is the fairly complex (to human ears) mixture of whistles,

trills, chirps, squawks, howls and screams that keeps pod members always in touch with one another and is probably necessary for successful pack hunting. The other is an echo-location noise, not unlike sonar and radar combined, which orients the animals in the water the way echo-location works for bats in the air. This also helps them locate prey.

But exactly how good, how efficient, are these whales at killing? They are agile and swift enough to catch an adult salmon in their short, sharp-pointed teeth set in jaws well developed for grasping a variety of food. Most warm-blooded prey, such as dolphins, porpoises, seals and sea lions, are swallowed whole if small enough; otherwise anything up to the size of gray whales may be torn apart and eaten piecemeal.

Here are some interesting feeding statistics from the northern Pacific area: One whale was observed catching and swallowing four porpoises in succession; another orca caught at sea had swallowed 13 porpoises, and another had 14 seals in its stomach. The latter orca was only 16 feet long. My friend Jeff Foott, a cinematographer, filmed killer whales snatching southern sea lions off Patagonia's beaches in Argentina. Killer whales in captivity, which may not need as much sustenance as wild ones, consume as much as 375 pounds of fish each day. Except for man, killer whales have no enemies.

The orca, or killer whale, is common in waters between Vancouver Island and the British Columbia mainland.

▼

There is only a single recent record of a killer whale attacking a human. In 1972, Hans Kretschmer was wearing a wet suit as he stretched out on his surfboard about 100 feet from shore off Point Sur, near Monterey, California. He felt something nudge his shoulder and saw only glossy black. At first he thought it was a huge shark that grabbed him, and he fought it with his fists. The creature backed away, and Kretchmer body-surfed to the beach. Later he needed 100 stitches to close the deep gashes on his thigh. The surgeon who stitched the leg had attended several shark victims previously, and he identified the wounds as positively inflicted by the teeth of an orca.

For more than two decades, biologists and whale researchers (now joined by a growing number of ordinary whale watchers) have worked in the Telegraph Cove–Johnstone Strait area because here the animals are relatively numerous, usually visible and not too difficult to approach. It is much easier than elsewhere to follow both the resident and transient pods that frequent Johnstone Strait. It is even possible to identify many individuals from the shape and markings on their dark dorsal fins. One thing the studies here have shown is that the local killer whales, unlike those in other areas of the world, tend to subsist far more on salmon and perhaps other fishes than on other sea mammals. They have even been observed in apparently "friendly" company with Dall porpoises and minke whales, which would normally be prey. The most surprising discovery at Johnstone Strait is the rubbing beach near Robson Bight. Orcas regularly come to this special place to roll on the smooth pebbles and rub their bodies in sandy patches to remove old, dead skin, an activity that underwater cameramen have often captured on film. We could have spent the rest of the summer following and photographing the sociable killers of Johnstone Strait, but too soon we were scheduled to head north again. No doubt we will return another year.

Orcas are most commonly seen in Antarctica and the eastern Pacific.

▲

The Kermode, or white bear, is an uncommon subspecies of black bear that lives on Princess Royal Island.

Another remarkable wildlife place along British Columbia's north coast is Princess Royal Island, a mountainous, forest-clad, granite land mass 50 miles long by 30 miles wide that rises out of the Pacific. A small number of Tsimshian natives live in seasonal communities around the island's fringe, making a living from the sea, but few ever penetrate far into the dark, roadless interior. Thus a population of white black bears and black gray wolves have lived almost unknown in the island's forests, which have not changed since the last ice age.

The bears, especially, are strange. Not southern polar bears, as was once reported, or albinos, they are a rare white or cream color phase of the same bear species that is black or brown elsewhere between Baja and Barrow. These Princess Royal bears (also called Kermode bears) have normal pigmentation, which can be seen in their eyes, skin and nose. Only their fur is light colored. But like too many uncommon animals, the threat of logging hangs over these ghost bruins. This area desperately needs protection by a provincial government that is too often unconcerned about conservation matters.

Passengers traveling north on ships of the Alaska ferry system can clearly see Princess Royal Island if they cruise past during daylight hours, but they will miss the Queen Charlottes, an archipelago of

▲

The wolves that inhabit Princess Royal
tend to be dark.

►

A gray wolf in British Columbia coastal
forest.

some 150 islands (six of them fairly large) and islets that lie out to sea well beyond regular shipping lanes. Sparsely populated by people, they are also blissfully distant from world problems, even though at the same latitude as Berlin, Amsterdam and Dublin. All these islands are good wildlife country.

The black bears of the Queen Charlottes are black. Black-tailed deer were introduced before 1900, and with abundant forage, mild winters and no predators, have prospered. Elk, raccoons, beavers, muskrats and (inadvertently) rats have also been introduced, not all of them wisely. Sleek sea otters swim in the surrounding waters, and a special island subspecies of the river otter lives on land. Half of British Columbia's sea lions haul out and breed on the archipelago. But gone—extinct—is the

▲

The Stellar's jay lives everywhere along the British Columbia coast. It is the official bird of the province.

◄

The great grey owl is the largest of those likely to be found along the Pacific coast.

►

Northern goshawk on Queen Charlotte Island.

dwarf, gray Dawson caribou that a handful of the very oldest residents might remember.

You cannot wander far in the lonely Queen Charlotte Islands without seeing some of the many bald eagles that nest here, or British Columbia's official bird, the Steller's jay. Next to the eagles, the Queen Charlotte goshawk is probably the most common raptor. Botanists have found at least six mosses and liverworts here that exist nowhere else.

Access to these lonely islands is by plane and ferry from Prince Rupert and Port Hardy on Vancouver Island. Those arriving in summer by boat might occasionally be startled by what resembles an uncharted reef ahead. It always turns out to be a vast raft of moon, or sail, jellyfish drifting just below the surface. When hundreds of thousands of these three-inch-long jellyfish are washing ashore, they resemble a fresh snowfall and are as slippery as wet ice.

Katmai N.P.
Kamishak Bay
Cook Inlet
ANCHORAGE
Kenai Fjords National Park
Afognak Island
Prince William Sound
Kodiak Island
Montague I.
KODIAK
Wrangell-St. Elias N.P.
Yakutat Bay
Alsek R.
Dry Bay
Glacier Bay N.P.
JUNEAU
Chichagof Island
Admiralty I.
SITKA
Baranof Island
Prince of Wales I.

Alaska

An Alaska River Odyssey

We ended our exploration of coastal British Columbia and entered Alaska in a roundabout way, by flying to Whitehorse, Yukon Territory, and near there, embarking on one of the great adventures of a lifetime. It was somewhat similar, but in reverse, to the sockeye salmon migration from the Pacific to Chilko Lake.

It was mid-morning when we rounded a bend of the mist-enshrouded river and dug our paddles deep into the cold, gray current. For a moment, all paddlers were too preoccupied to notice the huge animal standing on the bank, but suddenly all eyes focused on a dark grizzly bear that stood on its hind legs for a better look at us through seemingly myopic eyes.

The bruin was confused. First it galloped downstream as if to stay well ahead of the rafts. Then abruptly it turned around and waded a few feet out into the water for another look. Clearly it had never seen people riding in inflatable craft on its river before. The animal woofed softly, hesitated, and then evaporated into the evergreen forest not far away.

"That loud thumping I hear," someone commented, "is my own pulse pounding."

We were floating the Alsek River with 16 companions and four guide-boatmen. This sudden encounter with a grizzly on the first day was merely the first of 30-odd such meetings, none threatening, that we would have during the next 12 days. But the bears were only a part of what would make this trip one of our greatest episodes in a lifetime devoted to adventure and wildlife photography.

▲

A cloud spills over Johns Hopkins Glacier in Glacier Bay National Park.

The Alsek is one of two rivers (the Tatshenshini is the other) that originates in Canada's Yukon, hurries through Kluane National Park and the northwesternmost part of British Columbia, then flows into Glacier Bay National Park, Alaska, before emptying into the Gulf of Alaska at remote Dry Bay. With its many tributaries it is one of the world's most spectacular river systems, but nevertheless remains almost unknown. For 185 miles the Alsek slices—and we rafted—a channel that cuts through Pacific coastal mountains of the Saint Elias and Fairweather ranges, where summits rise to over 19,000 feet and include Mount Logan, Canada's highest peak.

Enroute we glided and sometimes splashed through whitewater past six biogeographic zones, one of which contains the world's largest non-polar glacial system; the last is a coastal rainforest. All the way it is unadulterated wilderness. We re-entered British Columbia but crossed no roads, saw no dwelling, found only a crumbling trapper's shack abandoned long ago, and saw no other humans. We did pass a dozen glaciers that calved at or near river's edge and we saw much wildlife in addition to the bears. And no wonder: no waterway on earth still wanders so far through pure wilderness on this crowded planet. For all of us it was like traveling through prehistory, and through primeval grandeur.

The journey began at Haines Junction, midway on the Alaska Highway, about 80 miles west of Whitehorse, Yukon's capitol. There, beside the Dezadeash River, rafts were inflated, life jackets fitted properly, and we were briefed on river running safety and procedure on water only a few degrees above freezing. Then we launched downstream, soon joining the Alsek River. Our goal was the Pacific Ocean, which we planned to reach in less than two weeks.

For all but two of the boatmen there was a special thrill in beginning this adventure. Unlike floating the Tatshenshini River (the "Tat") to the southeast, which is much better known among river runners, probably fewer than a hundred people had floated the entire length of the Alsek before this Canadian River Expeditions trip. That added an aura of discovery to the venture.

That first day we traveled only ten miles or so through Dezadeash Flats, where a moose grazed on ripening mountain avens and snow-covered ranges loomed high on both sides of us. No one lingered long around the campfire that first night. Instead all

▲
An unnamed glacier on the lower Alsek River near Windy Craggy mine site.

▲
An iris near the mouth of McNeil River.

▲

Brown bear and cubs dig for mussels at water's edge, and then climb onto the rocky shore at Glacier Bay.

turned in early for a night in tents pitched among old wolf tracks at woodland's edge. The next morning, a soft golden sunrise over a flat-calm river inspired a few of the earliest risers to dig cameras from their duffel bags.

During the following few days we established the rhythm that would continue throughout the journey. We stopped often to explore and to gather driftwood that would fuel the evening's cooking fire. Everywhere we paused there were abundant signs of wildlife: a wolverine, beaver cuttings and the pellet droppings of ptarmigan and moose, wolf and grizzly tracks, often one set on top of another. Once we found a rubbing tree where bear hairs had recently been left behind in the rough bark of a cottonwood. Following a short, fast run through rapids on the third evening, we camped just across the Alsek from Lowell Glacier. Huge blue bergs from the glacier floated on the river nearby, and all night long we could hear the grinding roar of the crumbling ice mass.

Soon after a breakfast big enough for twice as many, our trip leaders led us on a steep hike onto nearby Goatherd Mountain. (This monolith is unique in that it has a formal name; many other mountains and glaciers that would be landmarks elsewhere remain unnamed here.) The climb was an excellent opportunity for all to watch and photograph the bands of white mountain goats that spend summers on these precarious slopes. Goatherd is also the northernmost point where this rugged species survives.

Day five will not soon fade from anyone's memory. While eating breakfast beneath a large tarpaulin, protected from a steady rain, we watched a grizzly (number seven so far) stroll past camp. This one seemed unconcerned over the strangers in its wilderness and of their riveted interest in it. When the rain stopped we loaded the rafts and began an almost surreal passage through Lowell Lake and a phalanx of towering icebergs, many grotesque in shape and color. Some of the bergs were

floating and some were grounded on sandbars by the low Alsek River levels of late summer. It was—
is—hard to believe that such a polar spectacle exists only a few air hours from Seattle or Vancouver.
We have never seen anything to match it except in Antarctica, a half a world away.

Below Lowell Glacier, the river current gathers speed, and as we passed the scenery on both sides
of us more swiftly, so did it become more awesome. Midway in the trip, just after skimming past a
mother grizzly bear with twin cubs, standing on hind legs to stare at us in total disbelief, we came to
the second-fastest stretch of whitewater on the Alsek. Technically speaking, it is a Class IV rapids, not
to be taken lightly. To reconnoiter the 600-yard-long stretch, a guide made the run in one raft, without
passengers. Satisfied it was navigable, all who wished could have chosen to ride the other rafts, or walk
around the rapids and risk running into bears instead.

Just downstream we made camp in an absolutely idyllic setting. Hemmed in by the Saint Elias
Mountains, we pitched tents near the base of a 100-foot waterfall. The tracks of two wolves passed
where we drove our tent stakes into the ground. Some travelers bathed, hurriedly, in the natural
waterfall shower. Most waited for a portable shower tent to be erected and for water to be heated on
driftwood fires.

▲

Grizzly bear on a gravel bar of the Alsek–Tatshenshini River near the Alaska–British Columbia border.

There was a bittersweet, or maybe simply bitter, mood in camp on our ninth evening. Not far from where we sat around the campfire, and through binoculars watched a grizzly digging for edible roots, stood enormous Windy Craggy Mountain. If all would go as planned, a Toronto-based company would soon level off the entire crest of Windy Craggy and excavate an enormous open pit copper mine. To do so, they would build a network of roads, construct housing and cause environmental destruction difficult to comprehend. This would also end river running on this magnificent river system—just for a metal ore already in oversupply worldwide. We paddled downstream the next morning thinking we might be among the last to see this world-class wilderness intact.

(At least some news is good today. Just before I sat down to write this, word came that the British Columbia government, bending to pressure from many sources, had withdrawn all permits to mine Windy Craggy. Hopefully the withdrawal is permanent.)

We passed Walker Glacier, and then Alsek Glacier that impounds Alsek Lake, larger and choked with more massive icebergs than those that bobbed in Lowell Lake far upstream.

If anything, this portion of the Alsek-Tatshenshini that cuts through Glacier Bay National Park was even more magnificent than what we had already seen. The river here is a conduit that funnels humidity in from the sea. Where the river's upstream banks had been nearly barren, those here are dense with willows and fireweed, with spruce, cottonwoods and hemlock. Low clouds hang over the water, sometimes obscuring and sometimes exposing the mountains. Here, too, there is a dramatic change in the wildlife, a change that parallels the alteration in vegetation.

We had seen our last grizzly on the shore of Alsek Lake, but here bald eagles, terns and gulls circled overhead. And the dark faces we saw in the milky current ahead of us were harbor seals hunting for salmon.

▲

Alaskan brown bear with cubs near the McNeil River.

Early in the afternoon of our final day, in golden sunshine, we scraped ashore at Dry Bay, Alaska. The world's greatest ocean was within view. Dry Bay has a permanent year-round human population of five or six, and in summer a small salmon cannery operates there. A dirt airstrip has been scraped from the brush. The first person we met, the first human other than those of our little group that we had seen in two weeks, was the U.S. Customs officer, who is also the local game warden and national parks ranger. He welcomed us and bemoaned the fact that he could not make exactly the same trip we had made. We were in Alaska, the Great Land.

Alaska's Bear Coast

day is breaking slowly along the lonely southwestern Alaskan coast. A dense fog rolls in from the cold Bering Sea and across Shelikof Strait. But from the deck of the *R/V Waters*, anchored in Hallo Bay, I can clearly see the dark form of a large brown bear near the mouth of a stream on the beach only 300 yards away. It is extreme low tide, and the bruin is busy digging deep for clams. At times, only its rump is visible.

"That fog might lift," skipper Mike Park predicts, "by the time we have finished breakfast. Then we can go ashore for a closer look."

Peggy and I gulp a meal that is really too good not to savor, pull on hip boots, load cameras, lenses and tripods into backpacks and help lower the small skiff that will take us to shore. Our guide, bear biologist Polly Hessing, checks a 12-gauge shotgun to see that there are rifled slugs in the magazine and chamber. My pulse is racing because suddenly the fog really is lifting. Mike starts the outboard and, with friends Bob and Evelyn Mauch, we motor slowly toward the flat, sandy beach.

Now the bear we had watched from the boat is watching us, but it is no longer alone. Two others are standing just inland beside a shallow stream, and all three study us as our boat scrapes gravel. We step out to drag it farther onto solid ground. We go slowly, making no sudden moves, so as not to alarm the bears, or maybe it's the other way around. I extend the legs of my tripod and secure a 600mm lens to my 35mm camera. That's when the damp and dreary Alaskan scene suddenly comes alive.

The clam-digging bear is running away from us. But the other two are splashing at full speed in our direction. I see Polly start to raise the shotgun. For an instant I wonder what I'm doing in this godawful situation. Then as suddenly as they had begun their race toward us, the bears stop and pounce into the middle of a school of salmon. One comes up with a fish from which the bright red roe squirts. The other splashes away in another direction, still running down escaping fish.

When my pulse returns to normal I realize I have not taken a single picture of the extraordinary action. Neither has Peggy. Polly lowers the gun, takes a deep breath, and lets it out as a "Whew!"

But this is one of those happiest of expeditions when wildlife photographers have many more chances. During the next hour or so, as an incoming tide brings new schools of humpback salmon into their traditional spawning stream, we stand and shoot pictures of the fishing bears as fast as we can load, unload and reload film.

It is not a heavy run of fish, and the bears must work hard—frantically—to catch

Alaskan brown bears eating salmon.

▼

▲
Brown bear licks its paw after eating salmon.

►
Humpback salmon spawning in the vicinity of Valdez, Alaska.

even a few. But that works to our advantage. The bears race back and forth, sometimes not 50 feet from us. One bear sits in the sand, skins and eats a salmon barely 30 feet away from us. Neither bear seems to regard the four humans standing together as anything other than inanimate parts of the landscape.

The fishing ended at about the same time as the ocean tide began its long retreat and our supply of film was exhausted. The bears vanished with full bellies into the jumble of bleached driftwood that marked the high tide line on shore. We returned to the *Waters* to unwind. What we had just photographed would rank with our finest wildlife experiences.

The adventure had begun when Bill de Creeft telephoned us on a gloomy day in mid-winter. Bill is owner of a small fleet of floatplanes that, from a base in Homer, serves such scattered outposts of southwestern Alaska as Kodiak Island, the McNeil River, Katmai National Park and the entire Alaska Peninsula. This vast region comprises one of the last and largest wildernesses left on earth. The section of Alaskan coast that extends for 400 miles from Cook Inlet to Cold Bay, for example, contains not a single permanent year-round human settlement. Instead, the stretch of coast belongs to sea birds and sea lions, to eagles, whales and sea otters. And of course to brown bears that (at least in summer) might be properly called sea bears.

"A lot of that coast," de Creeft said on the telephone, "hasn't really been well explored. I *know* that plenty of brownies spend the summers in the sheltered bays along the beach and on the hundreds of streams where salmon spawn. Some of that country lies within the most-remote, least-known section of Katmai National Park where the bears are not hunted and some have never seen a human. Wouldn't it be great to cruise that area, to hunt those bears with a camera?"

What de Creeft was actually saying was that he had a boat, the *R/V* (for Research Vessel) *Waters*, available. Built in 1943 to serve as an Army tugboat, the 75-foot, wooden *Waters* was later and long used for Alaskan maritime research by such agencies as the National Park Service, the National Geographic Society and the Smithsonian Institution. But as research funds dried up it had recently been converted to a six-passenger-three-crew vessel for summertime ecotouring and bear watching trips. Bill had no trouble selling us on an exploratory trip.

In mid-July we flew about 90 minutes by Otter floatplane from Homer—past volcanic, steaming Augustine Island, Cape Douglas and the McNeil River State Sanctuary—to a rendezvous with the *Waters*, moored in Kukak Bay. A few minutes after the plane lifted off to return to Homer, a bear appeared, foraging along the rocky shore. We lowered the skiff, hoping for a closer look, but this bruin was super-shy. It vanished into the alders almost before we were underway.

That night the too-typical Alaskan weather closed in. Rain pelted the boat, and a savage wind almost tore the *Waters* from her anchorage. But dawn broke clear and we spent the next two weeks exploring one of the most scenic, and at times one of the most intimidating, coastlines in the world.

From Kukak Bay, which is really a deep, green fjord, we cruised past islands carpeted with bodies of hauled-out Steller's sea lions, past great rafts of black-legged kittiwakes, guillemots, glaucous-winged gulls, and entered Kaflia Bay. At the head of

▲
An American mink watches photographers shooting bears.
▼
Steller's sea lions approach our boat off Marmot Island.

▲

Large chunks of ice float in the water of Tracy Arm, the product of "calving" at the base of Sawyer Glacier in southeast Alaska.

Kaflia we filmed our first bears, a pair of small ones that stalked the Dolly Varden trout that seemed abundant in a very shallow stream. When the bears went elsewhere someone rigged a spinning rod and caught enough of the trout for dinner. He needn't have. Bottom fishing from the stern of the *Waters*, the second mate had boated two halibut, one of which weighed about 75 pounds. No seafood is more delicious than halibut fresh from the cold ocean floor.

From Kaflia we headed southward again, passing Kinak Bay, Takli Island and many more noisy sea lion colonies, into Amalik Bay and through a narrow channel into Geographic Harbor, named by the National Geographic Society during a first exploration of that magnificent place. We saw no bears here, but everywhere we walked on shore we found their tracks, as well as those of wolves and foxes among the fireweed and other wildflowers. On a sunny day the mountain scenery was simply

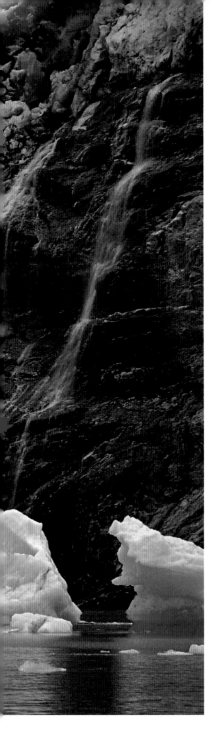

▲

Stellar's sea lions hauled out at Afognak
Island.

▶

Foxes are common on the wild shorelands
of Alaska.

incredible. Bald eagles nested on many orange, lichen-covered, large
rocks not connected to the shore.

We found our greatest bear bonanza by far in Hallo Bay, where
snow-capped Mount Steller, Kukak Volcano, Hallo Glacier and Devil's
Desk peak always loomed ominously in the background, and where at
least a dozen streams drained into Shelikof Strait. From our anchorage
in the lee of Ninagiak Island we could always look ashore through
binoculars and spot a number of active bears.

Our first morning on the beach of Hallo Bay we met close up—
too close for comfort, it seemed at first—the dark brown female
someone named Dolly. Compared to most of the other bears, Dolly

▲

Alaskan brown bears courting, not fighting, on the beach at Hallo Bay, Katmai. This is high among the most exciting things we have ever seen.

seemed thin. But no other bears we met were as lively or as agile. Every bear has a different fishing technique, and some are far more successful fishers than others. What Dolly lacked in skill she made up in speed, stamina, and distance covered in running down scattered salmon schools.

One day Dolly suddenly ran away altogether, and coming up behind us was the reason. Or two reasons. A pair of huge brownies moved toward us and into the streams at a fast pace. Right away we could see that their intentions were not directed toward fishing, but in mating. Dancing, chasing and pawing one another while standing ten feet tall on their hind legs, the pair gave us the most exciting as well as the most tense moments of our trip. We called the lovers Fred and Ginger, after Fred Astaire and Ginger Rogers, who danced their way to fame in the films of the 1940s. I still think of our pair of impassioned bears this way.

For a time the two seemed not to notice us at all. But then Fred looked our way and seemed to discover some problem. Forgetting his amorous thoughts for the moment, he began to stalk purposefully in our direction. Ginger went the other way.

When he was so close that we could hear his quick breaths, Fred looked around and realized that love was vanishing in the distance. His second thought convinced him that Ginger's idea was better than his own, and he turned away to follow her. I later paced off the distance that had separated us by measuring from the great footprints he left in the soft sand. It was 60 feet.

The next day the courting couple was back on the scene again, this time mixing fishing with frolicking. Again Fred came close, and we could clearly see a deep red gash on his foreleg, proving that bear romance can get rough.

Thanks to Fred and Ginger, as well as some of the other bruins we met, I am convinced of one important fact. No bear photography we have ever done pumped so much adrenalin into my system so quickly as did that episode on the shore of Hallo Bay. Nor, incidentally, did we ever shoot so much film in so short a time as here along Alaska's brown bear coast.

This bear coast, or south coast of Alaska, begins almost at the British Columbia border. It ends over 1,000 miles due west near Cold Bay, at the tip of the Alaska Peninsula. To explore, even just to step ashore on every one of the islands, large and small, that lie along the shoreline would require a

Alaskan brown bears courting.

lifetime of the highest adventure. Just offshore, a traveler might encounter ten species of the world's great whales—possibly during a single, long summer's day. The island names alone conjure in the mind excitement and mystery: Revillagigedo, Prince of Wales, Baranof, Hinchinbrook, Shuyak, Trinity, Semidi, Shumagin, Deer. The wildlife and geography of all are simply magnificent, but endemic foul weather, icy water and isolation do not make the exploration easy or inexpensive. Over the years, however, Peggy and I have plugged away at it. Most recently we cruised what may be the most striking area in all of southeastern Alaska on another boat, the *M/V Wilderness Explorer*.

Measuring 112 feet (the length of a large blue whale), weighing 98 tons (or the same as three large humpback whales) and with a capacity of 36 passengers, the *Wilderness Explorer* is any green, or ecotourist's, best bet, for security and comfort, to venture silently into southeast Alaska's deep fjords. The ship is also an ideal platform for wildlife watching and photography. The *Wilderness Explorer* is large enough to carry inflatable rafts and a flotilla of sea kayaks to carry passengers ashore anywhere they choose. I think of the ship as the ideal wilderness base camp.

We boarded the *Explorer* late on a gray June evening in Juneau, where giant cruise ships were

spilling less fortunate passengers onto crowded docks. At dusk, beyond the last lights blinking through a drizzle on shore, we cruised southward via Stephen's Passage past Taku Inlet and into the short summer night.

The romance ends as the female strolls off into the sunset.

Early the next morning we were suddenly awakened by thunder, followed by the rolling of our boat. I quickly pulled on my pants and stepped out onto the wet deck to find that we had anchored near the base of a great glacier towering 250 feet above us. The top of the glacier was strangely aglow in weak, morning sunlight. The base was still in shadow and a luminous blue. The "thunder" that aroused us was the sound of "calving," when huge chunks of ice break off the face of the glacier and crash into the sea, creating enormous swells. The broken pieces dot the area as icebergs of all sizes, on which harbor seals haul out.

The rich smell of the sea hung in the air. Glaucous-winged gulls circled and screamed above; pigeon guillemots and scoters swam among the ice floes around the vessel. Altogether, Sawyer Glacier, here at the termination of Tracy Arm, was a wild scene no one on board is likely to forget. The looming southeast Alaska scene was even more spectacular looking straight up from the low-riding kayaks that we soon launched.

There are many scenes similar to this one in southeast Alaska, which comprises a thin coastal strip and the Alexander Archipelago of islands that begins at the southern end of Prince of Wales Island (and the British Columbia border) and ends about 550 miles northwest of Icy Bay, where vast Malaspina Glacier approaches the Gulf of Alaska. Most of this region, distinguished by its year-round wetness, is wilderness. The human population is low. Except for the blue-white glaciers that originate hundreds of miles away in Canada, the land is green, lush, and if you do not relish wildness, intimidating. Summers are cool, winters are relatively mild, and rainfall varies from 50 to 200 inches a year.

America's largest national forest, the Tongass, makes up 75 percent of southeast Alaska, or about 16.8 million acres. Within Tongass, the world's largest temperate rainforest, remain some of the largest tracts of virgin old-growth woodlands left in the United States or, for that matter, anywhere. But logging has already taken a terrible toll in large sections of the Tongass and continues inexorably. To preserve portions of wild southeast Alaska for all times, 21 wilderness areas have been designated by the United States Congress. Best known of these are Misty Fjords and Admiralty national monuments, and Glacier Bay National Park

The biggest unlogged portion of southeast Alaska survives now in the Alexander Archipelago, where the lush forests support many wildlife species, including some rare and disappearing ones. Higher densities of brown bears and bald eagles exist here, especially on Admiralty Island, than anywhere else. Among the other predators are wolves (but only in two places: the mainland from Glacier Bay to Yakutat, and islands

Early morning entrance to Tracy Arm,
Glacier Bay. The weather here is too
often damp and misty, but the scenery
is awesome nonetheless.

▼

such as Prince of Wales, south of Frederick Sound), wolverines, mink, river otters and martens. Any southeast island with brown bears supports no wolves or black bears, although all three species share habitats elsewhere in Alaska. Biologists are uncertain whether this is an accident of geography or a result of species conflict. Other inhabitants of the old-growth forests include Sitka black-tailed deer, mountain goats, spawning salmon, goshawks and sharp-shinned hawks, great horned and sawhet owls, woodpeckers, winter wrens, Townsend's warblers, red-breasted nuthatches, flycatchers, Steller's jays, brown creepers, golden-crowned kinglets and marbled murrelets. Although they are sea birds, the latter require the crowns of intact forests inland for nesting, and these, like too many forest areas, are greatly threatened. Although marbled murrelets are widespread in southeast Alaska, numbering about 25,000, only one nest has ever been found here. Made of thick moss, the nest was 50 feet above ground in a mountain hemlock on Baranof Island, three-quarters of a mile from the sea.

A varied community of rodents climb in the trees and scamper over the old-growth forest floors. Largest of the rodents are the porcupines. Red squirrels and northern flying squirrels come next. By far the most abundant rodent is the northern red-backed vole, which exists in greatest numbers where there are plenty of deadfalls and rotting logs for cover. We spotted a good many of the voles scurrying about in the forests at Point Adolphus and, later, at Glacier Bay's Bartlett Cove.

The old-growth forests of southeast Alaska that still survive are absolute marvels of nature. They are multi-storied, containing trees of all ages; many are 300 years old, the oldest exceed 800 years. The total mass weight of plant life in a mature southeastern Alaskan forest is many times

Harbor seals haul out on icebergs in Tracy Arm.
▼

that of the densest Amazon rainforest. Because of the dampness, forest fires never burn here. Individual Sitka spruces tower 200 or more feet tall and measure ten feet in diameter. With so few of these remaining, it seems a criminal act to cut more for any reason. They are irreplaceable. The *Wilderness Explorer* gave us a good chance to see some of Alaska's precious forests, both from a distance and to walk, with difficulty, on the soggy ground beneath the canopy of trees.

From Tracy Arm we turned northwest overnight, around the northern end of Admiralty Island, into Icy Strait, to eventually drop anchor at daybreak in Mud Bay, just west of Point Adolphus, a place that has suddenly become well known, and with good reason, for its whale watching. In summer, humpback whales congregate in this vicinity to feed in the nutrient-rich waters. Minke and killer whales might also be seen here.

Humpbacks are powerful long-distance travelers. Mature males and females weigh 35 to 40 tons. Every fall, after fattening in southeast Alaskan waters, the 350 or so resident humpbacks travel non-stop to calving and breeding grounds in Hawaii. Reproduction accomplished, they return to cooler Alaskan waters in May or early June, where they remain until November. Humpbacks are extremely and understandably popular with whale watchers and cameramen because they are the most acrobatic and most visible of all the world's whales, especially when feeding—and they have a lot of feeding to do. On their return to Alaskan waters, they have lost as much as a quarter of their body weight, or from eight to ten tons.

Now the whales use different and exciting (at least to serious whale watchers) means to regain the lost weight. Cruising on the ocean surface is their basic feeding routine. Mouths wide open, they suck up massive amounts of food-laden seawater. The food is usually krill—small shrimp-like crustaceans—or small fishes. When the whale presses its tongue to the roof of its mouth, all the water is expelled through baleen plates, which act as a strainer, leaving the food behind. Baleen is the same material that forms the hoofs of muskoxen and human fingernails; it hangs from the upper jaw into the whale's mouth like a long, coarse fringe.

Humpbacks also do what has been called "bubblenet feeding." First they dive downward in a spiral, leaving behind a circular wall of bubbles—a sort of natural net—that seems to concentrate prey. The diving whales then switch ends and explode back up to the surface through the center of their bubble "nets," their jaws agape. At times several humpbacks cooperate in this endeavor, and the resulting turbulence wouldn't be a good place to be caught in a sea kayak.

Early in the morning, several small pods of humpbacks were very active near Point Adolphus, some feeding on the surface fairly near to the anchored *Wilderness Explorer*. We had the option of trying to photograph them from the vessel's deck or from a much lower, more dramatic angle in a kayak. We selected the deck for its greater stability as a camera platform, and that proved to be a mistake. During the next few hours, a few whales did occasionally breach (jump clear or partially clear of the water surface), blow and show their huge tails before diving in the general vicinity of the ship, but the kayakers had a much better look at them. Some felt the whales had approached too near for comfort.

From Point Adolphus and the humpbacks it was only a short run across Icy Strait to the entrance of Glacier Bay. Had we arrived here with the discoverer Captain George Vancouver in 1794, only 200 years ago, we would have found no Glacier Bay at all. At that time Icy Strait was choked with ice, and most of what is Glacier Bay National Park today was then covered by a single glacier over 4,000 feet thick, about 20 miles wide, and which extended inland more than 100 miles into the Saint Elias Mountain Range.

Humpback whale surfaces at Point Adolphus, and swims toward the Wilderness Explorer.

▼

The immense change since then is difficult to comprehend, and the changes are
ongoing, because the glacier continues to melt. During a visit in 1879, the California
naturalist John Muir found that the face of the ice had retreated almost 50 miles since
Vancouver's visit, and since then it has withdrawn another 25 or so miles. In the wake
of the retreat are some of the most striking scenes of "smaller" tidewater glaciers and
deep fjords, of lonely islets and glistening ice floes, of sheer beauty and green forest
regrowth on the face of the planet. There is also a surprising amount of wildlife; many species are
increasing as forests gradually grow out of the snouts of retreating ice fields.

▲

Johns Hopkins Glacier in Glacier Bay.

◄

A humpback whale breaches at Point
Adolphus, near the mouth of Glacier Bay.

My first visit to Glacier Bay in the late 1960s was a rugged experience of camping near Bartlett
Cove, where rain fell almost every day. But hiking the nearby trails, where I rarely met another human,
was a crash course in how temperate rainforests grow out of glacial till. Areas left bare by ice 25 years
earlier were covered with alder-willow thickets. After 50 years, these thickets were topped by
cottonwood trees and a few evergreens. After a century, the mixed cottonwood and spruce forests were
approaching almost 100 feet tall. The oldest forests at Glacier Bay were mostly spruce.

It was on that first Glacier Bay visit, on the beach, when photographing scarlet paintbrush and
chocolate lilies growing among the coarse grasses, that I found my first brown bear tracks etched in
tidal muck, and a few minutes later met the tracks' maker. I am certain that bruin clearly saw me
standing motionless, weak in the knees, but it gave no sign of recognition whatever as it walked past
me toward Point Gustavus.

Later that same morning I watched a more familiar creature, a coyote. This animal, like others
of its species, a survivor of a constant battle with humanity, kept its distance from me. It seemed to be
foraging for whatever was washed ashore with the tide. On this more-recent trip into Glacier Bay,

▲

Northern hawk owl on southeastern Alaska forest.

◀

Paintbrush brightens the beach at Bartlett Cove, Glacier Bay.

aboard the *Wilderness Explorer*, we learned that no coyotes or any sign of them have been seen in the area since 1993. But now wolves are also appearing to replace them. There is no pattern or schedule, as with plants, by which animals colonize lands exposed by retreating glaciers. Plant seeds and spores can be carried by wind, waves and birds, but mammals have to reach colonization sites on their own, usually by walking or swimming.

From the deck of the *Wilderness Explorer*, we saw mountain goats on sheer rock walls of fjords where outcrops of green vegetation provided browse. Through binoculars, we watched as a dark animal standing in an alder thicket on shore became a cow moose. Approaching the Marble Islands, which contained rookeries of pelagic cormorants and glaucous-winged gulls, marbled murrelets surfaced near the ship. We cruised past more humpback whales and harbor porpoises to where more than a hundred Steller's sea lions hauled out on a rocky shore. The *Explorer* slowed and then stopped, idling just offshore where a light-colored female brown bear with twin cubs was foraging, scraping mussels from the rocks at waterline with her long, powerful foreclaws. We have photographed brown bears eating everything from clams and sockeye salmon to cow parsnip and new green grass, but never before had we seen them crunching down mussels.

We found large communities of sea otters, some of them females with small pups, rafting in dense beds of kelp near the Inian Islands. Not too many years ago, we would have found no otters

Red foxes are commonly seen, and often unwary, all along the Alaska coast.

here at all. The fur of a 60- to 80-pound adult contains almost 500,000 hairs per square inch, which insulates them for a lifetime spent almost entirely in cold saltwater. This fur was considered "soft gold" by hunters who almost eliminated the species from its entire range.

One gray but memorable morning, we turned into a narrow, misty inlet to suddenly face Johns Hopkins Glacier, one of the most-awesome features of the entire national park. The glacier itself seemed to flow in a double zig-zag pattern down to tidewater. Hundreds of harbor seals slept and floated on icebergs that bobbed near the glacier's base, and above them hovered terns and black-legged kittiwakes. We watched this scene for a long time, wishing for sunshine to bathe it in brighter light, but felt extremely fortunate to have seen it at all.

We ended our cruise on the *Wilderness Explorer* at Bartlett Cove, where barn swallows nested beneath the timbered dock, and two bald eagles perched nearby. The eagles, which had elicited great excitement early in the trip, now went almost unnoticed, their creaking cries a familiar background noise. Before catching a quick flight back to Juneau, we paused another night at the Glacier Bay Lodge, where a hen spruce grouse tended to new chicks outside our window.

• • •

Now pick up a map of Alaska and, from Glacier Bay, draw a line almost directly westward. You will cross the Gulf of Alaska and then the southwestern tip of the Kenai Peninsula. Continue just south of Augustine Island, a volcano that expels a breath of steam most of the time, and enter Kamishak Bay. At the farthest west end of the bay is McNeil Cove and the mouth of the McNeil River.

We have seen the vast penguin rookeries of Antarctica and the wildebeest migrations across the

Serengeti Plain, but neither of these exactly matches the wildlife spectacle that takes place each summer here in this total wilderness where the McNeil pours into the sea. We are not far from where this chapter about Alaska's bear coast began.

It is just after daybreak when we are awakened by the crunch of gravel outside our tent. Groggy at first, but then sitting upright in a warm sleeping bag, we carefully unzip the tent flaps and see the cruncher. A brown bear that may have weighed 800 pounds stands only 50 feet away.

For an instant the bruin stares back at us through small, brown eyes, puzzled and sniffing the damp Alaskan morning. Next the great animal rises onto its hind legs for a better look at the cluster of red and yellow nylon tents scattered among tussocks of tall Arctic grass. Viewed through flimsy mosquito netting, the standing bear is an awesome, unnerving sight. Without a sound, it drops to all fours and shuffles away, without a backward glance, across a vast tidal flat. We breathe normally again.

The time is mid-summer. The place is far out on the Alaska Peninsula where the McNeil River empties into a tidal lagoon of Shelikof Strait. We are camped here because this is the peak of the annual spawning migration of chum salmon up the river. Hundreds, probably thousands, of generations of brown bears have annually gathered here to gorge on the fish at a chasm—really a natural fish trap—called McNeil Falls. Ten of us have flown here by floatplane to watch and photograph this extraordinary event.

The unexpected bear visit in camp is reveille for everyone. We dress, pull on high waterproof boots and wolf down breakfast in a shack which, with the pit toilet some distance away, is the only permanent structure within 100 miles in any direction. With backpacks full of photographic gear, lunch and water, we strike out for the falls, an hour's hike from the campsite. Alaska ranger-biologist Larry Aumiller leads the single-file march.

It is not a gentle hike. First we wade across the lagoon, which is passable only during low tides. At the edge of the lagoon we see where brown bears have been digging tidal flats for clams. Huge paw prints are etched everywhere in the soft sand. Abruptly the trail turns from the mudflats and climbs a steep bluff where in places the grass is shoulder high. Visibility all around is zero. Twice Aumiller pauses and shouts to clear the trail of bears, which we can hear snort. We feel the prickle of new sweat when a female with cubs looms ahead and stares sullenly at us for a moment. But she retreats and we continue, now at a faster pace. Suddenly we reach a knoll overlooking one of the greatest of wildlife spectacles.

Below us tumbles McNeil Falls, a necklace of foaming green cascades choked with hook-jawed salmon in pinkish spawning colors. Gulls and bald eagles scream and dive above the fish. But we hardly notice the birds, so intent are we on the two dozen or so giant bears that are stalking, splashing, quarreling and feeding on the fish.

From all directions, bears are constantly arriving and leaving the bonanza on centuries-old trails. We affix cameras onto tripods and watch surly, aging males as well as young sows with very small spring cubs. Aumiller has seen one ancient, shaggy boar come to McNeil for 26 consecutive years. Each bear has a name: Gold, a sow with unusual yellow claws; White, one of three cubs first seen and named on the Fourth of July—the others are Blue and Red; Patches, whose hair grows unevenly, and Rusty, who has the disturbing habit of bringing his fish within a few yards of our viewing platform before eating it. Our favorite is Miss Mouse, an attractive mother of three with two small M-shaped scars on her muzzle.

▲

A brown bear eating salmon in the McNeil River.

▲

Two male grizzlies fight over the best fishing territory.

Some bruins are naturally expert fishermen that catch one salmon after another, almost effortlessly; others never seem to get the knack of it. But for five or six weeks, as long as the salmon spawn, the area just below McNeil Falls is an arena of drama and conflict. It is a place where camera film is exposed at an alarming rate.

▲

Alaskan brown bear cub initiates play with its mother.

No sanctuary in the world offers a better chance, and at such close range, to see in great numbers the largest living land carnivores. About a hundred brown bears frequent the area in summer, and as many as 50 of these may be seen at the water at one time. The 85,000-acre McNeil River State Game Sanctuary is carefully managed by the state of Alaska to assure the safety of the animals as well as the people who come from around the world to see them.

During the salmon run, only ten people are permitted access to the McNeil Falls area at one time. Since demand to visit is great and increasing, permits for four-day periods are awarded through an annual lottery.

The area is total wilderness. Biologist Aumiller and an assistant constitute the entire permanent summer population; in winter the area is uninhabited. There are no overnight facilities, and each visitor brings everything but the drinking water he will need to live for the four-day period. It is wise to bring extra food because foul weather can ground air transportation for several days at a time. A good, waterproof tent, warm clothing and rain gear are essential.

Over the years, McNeil's bears have been habituated to regard humans simply as parts of the landscape. They are never to connect thoughts of people with food, and no hunting is permitted. Human visitors are required to use only a single trail between the campsite and the designated bluff viewing site overlooking McNeil Falls. Bears expect to see people in these places and will ignore them, although a few may approach to what may be a heart-stopping distance. Any bruins that wander too close to the camping area are driven away with a shrill boat siren. There have been no incidents in the two decades that Alaska's Department of Fish and Game (with Larry Aumiller) have been in control.

A psychologist who visited McNeil noted that while watching the bears interact he had seen almost every aspect of human behavior mirrored in the bears. There was the greed of larger bears who, although they were already sated, stole salmon from smaller ones. There was also territoriality, mother love, pretense, anger, contentment (one old female sleeping on her back, belly full of fish), persistence (an aggressive mother determined to feed her cubs at any price), drive, covetousness, guile (one distracts another's attention long enough to invade its fishing hole), competition, thuggery (one cub takes another's catch by assault), encroachment (an old, past-prime bear is forced out of a favorite fishing spot), intimidation and harassment, all of it undisguised.

Certainly there is no wildlife adventure in Alaska, or anywhere else, exactly like an expedition to the McNeil River Sanctuary. It ranks high among the world's greatest wildlife attractions; places we must by all means preserve.

Large male bears fighting for territory on the banks of McNeil River.

▼

Alaska

Wildlife Beachheads in the Bering Sea

no written record survives today of a fateful morning in 1786 when a deck hand aboard a Russian sailing ship commanded by Gerasim Pribilof suddenly sighted land through dense gray mists. Surely the flocks of screaming seabirds had alerted the crew that a landfall was somewhere within reach. Probably the towering cliffs and tundra-covered cinder cones were first glimpsed at dangerously close range, because thick scud and fog are endemic in the cold Bering Sea.

After dropping anchor near enough to hear the bellowing of fur seal bulls on the beaches, Pribilof managed to go ashore on one (no one knows which) of the two islands later named St. George and St. Paul, there to stare in wonder and disbelief at the sight before him.

After a single-minded three-year search back and forth across one of the most turbulent seas in the world, the last and perhaps largest fur seal rookery on earth had been discovered. At that time in history it was like finding gold bullion piled high on the beach.

BARROW

Cape Prince of Wales

Kotzebue Sound

St. Lawrence Island

NOME

Norton Sound

Yukon Delta

St. Mathew I.

Nunivak Island

Kuskokwim Bay

St. Paul I.

Pribilof Islands

St. George I.

Bristol Bay

Alaska Peninsula

Unimak Island

COLD BAY

Andreanof Islands

Fox Islands

▲

Fur seal harem.

The slaughter of these Bering Sea mammals was similar to that of other fur seals as soon as men found them elsewhere on the globe. Here were untold riches—unlimited soft, golden pelts, for the easy taking. The wealth of the czar in Saint Petersburg was built on selling Russian fur elsewhere in Europe. Natives of the Aleutian Islands to the south were enslaved to kill and skin the seals for the Russians as quickly as possible. By 1834, the fur seals, like the walruses and sea otters before them, were all but wiped out. Taken were an estimated three million pelts worth from ten to 20 billion dollars at today's values.

Fortunately the combination of history, economics, logistics, the U.S. purchase of Alaska, and an international agreement signed in 1911 (and ratified in 1957) by Russia, Japan, Canada and the United States, guaranteed the survival of the northern fur seal, a species 30 million years old. Today, visitors to the Pribilof Islands can still see great herds of fur seals on those same beaches, where the sea mammals haul out each summer to give birth and then to breed again. Although the numbers are only a fraction of those found by the Russian captain, the sight is awesome nonetheless. Other than here, from May to August, fur seals are seldom seen alive except by a few commercial fishermen cruising from Alaska southward to the Oregon coast.

We first visited St. Paul, the larger of the islands, which hosts the larger number of fur seals, on a photographic assignment in 1974. We flew there from Anchorage and Cold Bay (on the tip of the Alaska Peninsula) via a vintage, less-than-luxurious DC-6 tailored more for carrying cargo than passengers. We descended through a hole in the overcast to a stark landscape where clumps of purple lupine, blown by wind and a stinging rain, were the tallest plants in view.

We seldom saw the sun during that first expedition but made plenty of footprints
lugging backpacks full of rain gear and photo equipment from one seal beach to
another. Every day brought fresh discovery, not only of the lively antics of mating fur
seals, but of steep sea cliffs that were alive and seething with tens of thousands of
nesting seabirds. Because of the long summer days and brief nights at that Arctic latitude, we slept very
little, using the extra hours exposing film. You have to see, hear and smell this spectacle to believe it.
So, at trip's end, despite the rotten weather, we resolved to return at the first opportunity.

That chance came in 1987. We were to shoot fresh photographs for a book about wilderness
Alaska. This time our destination was Saint George, the smaller of the two major Pribilofs. We flew
directly from Anchorage and arrived in time for lunch at the austere, wood frame St. George Hotel,
which was recently designated as a National Historic Landmark. After a five-minute walk from the
hotel, we were focusing cameras on puffins perched on dark sea cliffs just below us.

We soon realized that St. George has fewer fur seals than St. Paul, and some beaches that were
once alive with beachmaster bulls guarding large harems of cows are now nearly bare of the animals.
The seabird population is also down, although not so drastically. The types of nets and fishing
methods used today by large commercial fishing fleets, mostly from Asia, are causing the alarming
destruction. Still, for its size, St. George remains among the largest seabird colonies in the Northern

Northern fur seal rookery on St. Paul
Island in the Pribilofs.

Hemisphere and surely ranks among the world's premier bird sights.

In 1987, a million thick-billed murres, the largest colony in the North Pacific, nested on the island's cliffs as high as 1,000 feet above the pounding surf. St. George is probably the world's largest breeding site of the parakeet auklets, and a major nesting place of crested and least auklets. Almost the entire world population (95 percent) of red-legged kittiwakes, exhilarating but dizzying to watch on the sheer cliffs, nests here. We observed an agile Arctic fox climb directly down to capture a kittiwake nestling, to feed its own young hidden in a cliff-top den.

Three weeks later, toward the end of July, we were watching another fox, this time a thin red fox, robbing the nest of a black-legged kittiwake on another distant outpost, Round Island, in Bristol Bay of the Bering Sea.

Even among Alaska's teeming wildlife beachheads, Round Island is unique. One of the islands comprising the Walrus Islands State Game Sanctuary, and little more than two square miles in area, Round Island is the hauling-out place, the summer bachelor headquarters, for almost all of the world's male Pacific walruses. About 10,000 males gather here from June until August. They pack narrow gravel beaches as tightly as sardines in a can. These bulls average a ton and a half apiece and ten feet in length. Perhaps nowhere else, not even where vast herds of African elephants still roam, is so much biomass packed per acre onto so little solid ground. But only one or two humans, wildlife biologists, inhabit the islands, and only as custodians during the short "walrus summer."

▲ Parakeet auklets, St. George Island.

▲ Murres on nest cliffs, St. Paul Island.

◄ Black-legged kittiwake rookery.

Our "camp" was a two-person mountain tent pitched atop a cliff and facing the westward tip of the island, the only locality where landing is sometimes safe and which is near most of the walrus beaches. From this lonely site that foxes visited every day we could load our gear into backpacks and hike outward on the thin, steep, usually slippery trails that led to the bird cliffs and beaches. Just 30 minutes away, through coarse, thigh-high *Calamagrostis* grass and Arctic wildflowers, we could look down upon one beach where 800 bulls lolled in an area much smaller than a soccer field. Wall-to-wall walrus.

We did not look down upon a tranquil scene. Some bulls were leaving the haulout beach to feed at sea while others were returning, looking for a favorable spot to rest. Fights, some noisy and savage, broke out as the bulls jostled for position or just room to breathe. The walruses used their long ivory

▲

Male walruses, Round Island, Alaska.

◄

Two walrus bulls spar for dominance, or
maybe just for the practice.

►

Thousands of male walruses spend every
summer hauled out on Round Island.
The shores here are covered with one
huge, seething biomass.

tusks to jab neighbors into giving ground. From time to time we could even hear the strange
chiming—like piano chords played out of tune—that the walrus somehow make by expelling air in
shallow water. Scientists still do not understand this, but to us, filming from just above, the unreal
sound came loud and clear. And haunting.

We have spent many summers vagabonding the wild places of Alaska, which means we have
experienced our share of dismal, damp weather. That is one of the penalties exacted by this exquisite
part of the world. But on Round Island we were repaid, with interest, for all the foul weather of the
past; for five straight days we wallowed in warm sunshine under clear skies. Not one drop of rain fell
on our tent and, implausibly for wild Alaska, especially the Bering Sea region, we had to apply
sunscreen lotion to our bare arms and faces.

Our luck held until we descended the vertical cliff below our camp toward the beach, where bull
walruses cleared a path for us to reach a waiting dingy. We then transferred to a salmon fishing boat
that would take us to the mainland. From the boat deck we looked back on an incredible scene:
thousands of all-white kittiwakes nesting directly above thousands of walrus bulls whose massive
bodies flared blood red in the setting sun.

We later learned that just after our departure, and for the next eight days, violent storms prevented anyone from leaving or landing on remote Round Island.

To write that any of the islands of the Bering Sea are remote is an understatement. They are almost as unreachable now as when explorer Vitus Bering first explored those icy waters for Russia in 1741, years before Pribilof's voyage. On board his tall-masted ship was a German naturalist, Georg Steller. (The first bird Steller saw after landing on mainland Alaska was the handsome dark-blue jay that carries his name.) When a sudden onset of foul weather prevented Bering from returning to Kamchatka, he was forced to overwinter on a bleak island where many crew members died.

But the inquisitive Steller found huge sea mammals living and feeding on marine algae in the shallows all around. Unknown to this time, he gave the world its first and only description of this great northern sea cow, now known as Steller's sea cow. Adults measured more than 35 feet long and probably weighed three tons. Killing and eating them no doubt spared Bering and his entire crew from starvation that winter.

The sea cows, however, did not have long to survive on earth. Defenseless and unwary, they were slaughtered for meat and oil by crews of every ship that later sailed these waters. Only 27 years after

▲

The rarely photographed rock sandpiper, high on a St. George Cliff.

◀

Wooly lousewort and cow parsnip on St. George Island, Pribilofs.

their discovery, the last one was gone, exterminated almost before the world knew they existed. Sadly, some other sea mammals, such as Steller's sea lion, appear to be headed for the same fate, although more slowly. Their numbers are drastically down everywhere along the Pacific Coast, and in recent years they have altogether disappeared from some centuries-old haunts.

For 36 hours, a late winter snowstorm had raged over the Bering Sea, smothering still another island, lonely, isolated Nunivak, in a terrible whiteout. Visibility is zero, and the temperature is well below freezing. Until the storm ends, Peggy and I, together with four Inuit guides, are marooned—like marmots deep in a winter burrow—in a rude shack barely 20 feet square. A foot of hard, wind-blasted snow covers our sod-roofed refuge. Drifts pile up and seal the two small windows. We stay warm inside as long as the supply of driftwood, blown here from Siberia and gathered on the shore about a quarter of a mile away, lasts. When the fire dies, it is cold again.

In the last stages of acute cabin fever I grab a shovel to dig my way out. What I find is a shock—a brilliant, serene new world. The wind has nearly stopped blowing, and the pale, late-winter sun illuminates a silent white wilderness. Soon all of us are standing outside, first in disbelief, then excitement.

Someone suggests looking for muskoxen. Immediately we don our parkas, fur hats and mittens, dig our snowmobiles out from beneath deep drifts, and load camera gear onto the cargo sleds. We set out quickly, heading east along the steep, snow covered sand dunes that parallel Nunivak's southern shore.

Before long, Howard Amos, the lead Inuit guide, stops and points to dark forms moving in the distance. Through binoculars the forms become a herd of a dozen muskoxen that have also spotted us. They hesitate and then run a short distance to the top of the nearest knoll, where they stop and look back. Then, as muskoxen have done for thousands of years, the herd forms a protective circle, all the

adults facing outward. Motionless, they stare at us as we shoulder tripods and slowly approach on foot into camera range.

Although muskoxen (*Ovibos moschatus*) are not rare or endangered, seeing them in the wild, even in wild Alaska, means traveling to some of the most remote and uncomfortable places. Few non-natives ever see these animals in winter. Now we stand barely a hundred feet from a group, and we intend to take advantage of it in the fading Arctic twilight.

Through my viewfinder I focus on a magnificent, primeval sight. For the next hour, until the sun sinks behind the Bering ice pack in the west, we expose roll after roll of film from every conceivable angle, because we know that we many never see these animals like this again.

The *oomingmak* (meaning "bearded one") of the Inuit is a handsome animal. Its most striking feature is its pelage. Coarse, dark-brown guard hairs as long as three feet, easily the longest of any North American mammal, hang down to brush the snow or blow in the wind. Guard hairs also form beards, and, on males, dark mats that accentuate powerful shoulder humps. Beneath that coarse outer coat is a much finer, lighter-colored hair called *qiviut*, as soft as the finest cashmere and so thick that neither cold nor frost can penetrate it. Later on, as winter blends into spring, the muskoxen will shed their *qiviut*, an estimated four and a half pounds annually for each animal. As the shed wool works its way out through the guard hairs, the animals will look ragged, but as we see them now the herd is sleek and beautiful.

All muskoxen have horns, but those of the females are shorter and more slender than those of the bulls. Male horns have heavy bosses and are shaped like deeply drooping handlebar moustaches. One

bull's horns measure about two feet on each side. I cannot believe this animal probably weighs under 800 pounds and stands only five feet high at the hump. It looks massive, as large as any bison we may find in Montana.

But one fact impresses me much more than these statistics. Few large wild mammals anywhere, and none in North America, have been easier to photograph, once located, than this one. And of course that explains why muskoxen were eliminated from Alaska and nearly wiped out on the mainland of Canada almost a century ago. Short legs, not built for flight, make it impossible for muskoxen to outrun wolves. When pursued by wolves, their primary natural enemy, the animals in a herd instinctively bunch up in a tight defensive circle or semicircle, calves hugging their mothers' flanks, just as they did at our approach.

The muskoxen's defensive tactic guaranteed the species' survival on the Arctic steppes and tundra for a million years. Then the first explorers brought firearms into the far North. All at once it was easy for anyone to walk within rifle range and, while dogs kept the *oomingmak* in place, shoot an entire herd. Whole populations were eradicated throughout their circumpolar range. The last survivors on mainland Alaska, a band of about 18 near Chandalar Lake, were killed by meat hunters at least 100 years ago. All that we know about their existence is based on oral reports handed down by natives, and from scattered skeletal fragments occasionally discovered in the frozen ground.

Muskoxen would still not be browsing Alaska's Arctic tundra were it not for one E.W. Nelson, who was named first chief of the United States Bureau of Biological Survey (precursor of the U.S. Fish and Wildlife Service) in 1930. Nelson convinced Congress to appropriate $40,000 to reestablish muskoxen in Alaska. At that time, the onset of the Great Depression, it was an extraordinary amount of money for almost any purpose. Nelson used the funds to buy 34 muskoxen from Greenland, half of them bulls and all of them a different subspecies than the North American muskox. Critics pointed out that Canada was willing to sell animals of the same (Alaskan) subspecies for less than half that figure. But, for unknown reasons, Nelson persisted, and so began one of the most bizarre and perhaps the longest-distance transplant of large wild creatures ever made.

▲ Barrow's goldeneyes flush from the edge of the ice near Cold Bay.

▲ Red-throated loon on nest, Kodiak National Wildlife Refuge.

◄ A large, old bull muskox.

The Greenland animals traveled first by steamer ship to New York, where they were held in quarantine by the New York Zoological Society. The next lap was via freight train across America to Seattle. From Seattle a steamship carried them to Seward, Alaska, where they boarded yet another train bound for Fairbanks, where they remained "for observation" for several years.

The muskoxen might still be living near Fairbanks except that their handlers considered them an increasingly surly and expensive nuisance. The animals didn't enjoy being fenced in. So the now 31 animals boarded their final freight train bound for Nenana, where they transferred to one more steamship to Marshall, and then by a barge that towed them further down the Yukon River to its delta at Kotlik. It was only by the slimmest of margins that the muskox shipment made it to Nunivak at all.

A decrepit boat, the *Meteor*, hired to tow the barge on the final leg of the odyssey, came close to breaking up during a stormy passage across Etolin Strait. Crew members had to man pumps non-stop for 14 hours to reach the island. The barge began to disintegrate when it went aground in the surf. On July 17, 1936, six years and more than 10,000 miles after leaving Greenland, 31 muskoxen waded ashore on Nunivak.

The globe-trotting animals found the new home in Alaska to their liking. Though much of Nunivak is annually covered with deep snow—which muskoxen cannot tolerate—the oceanside cliffs and sand dunes, especially along the southern shore, are swept bare of snow by incessant winter winds, exposing edible vegetation.

Horned puffins nest in cliff crevices high above the sea, St. George Island.

▼

One week of wandering and exploring in Nunivak's wilderness areas produced one indelible memory after another. Because the animals are concentrated so near the coast, they were always easy to find. But whenever we turned the snowmobiles northward,

we instead encountered large herds of reindeer plowing the deeper snow for scarce food plants on a lunar landscape of volcanic cones and calderas. We watched one small band digging furiously on a white ridge high on Roberts Mountain, at 1,675 feet, the highest point on the island.

Another day we pushed westward, hugging the shore to where, in summer, the Binajoaksmiut River flows into the Bering Sea. I had landed by floatplane in this narrow inlet in July 1969 and had found the river swarming with a run of salmon and seabirds. The coarse grass along the banks was knee-deep then, but only a single male muskox was there to graze on it. I shot a few exposures of the animal before it wandered far away. On our visit in April 1989, however, the Binajoaksmiut was frozen solid enough for us to cross with our snowmobiles, and we found three muskoxen herds in the vicinity of its mouth.

One of these was a band of bachelor bulls. I will never forget finding them, because just as we did, the sun broke through a day-long overcast to spotlight the animals looking down on us from sandy, higher ground, hair coats blowing in the wind. Before the sun retreated into the clouds, the bulls had become so accustomed to our presence that they paid us little attention. One was so confident that it turned its back, walked a few yards away and began to paw the snow for something beneath to nibble on.

▲

Spectacled and king eiders are among the waterfowl that swim and feed in the open waters of Alaska's northwestern coast.

Especially in winter, Nunivak's muskoxen live in an environment as fantastic as it is harsh. Whenever the wind blows from the west or southwest, as is common, a jagged, jumbled ice pack many miles wide piles up against the shore. Often we found the animals at the very edge of the pack. Glaucous gulls and cormorants circled above the cracks and open channels in the pack ice. More than once we noticed Arctic foxes walking in muskox tracks, scavenging for anything washed ashore by the crunching, shifting ice, or searching for lemmings flushed from their subnivean tunnels by the hooves of the muskoxen. The only small birds we saw were a few McKay's buntings that may nest in Asia and winter on Nunivak.

While we explored, we watched for any newly born muskox calves. By the end of April, many if not most of the cows would be calving, but we figured we were two to three weeks ahead of the peak. On the final day of our adventure, we spotted a herd of nine animals already gathered in tight formation near the edge of a sea cliff. We paused just long enough to photograph them in this splendid setting, and then continued on our way. But looking back from a distance, someone counted ten not

nine in the herd. One was very small. Without doubt the little one had been standing directly beneath its mother, completely hidden by her skirt of flowing brown hair.

Until recently the muskox was a mysterious animal that nobody knew much about, except that it is a fine example of nature's ability to fill every niche on Earth with life. Muskoxen simply lived in places too remote, too bitter, and too lonely to be well studied or even observed very much. But now that has changed. Biologists are studying muskoxen in Canada and Greenland, as well as in Russia and other places that have been repopulated with animals from the Nunivak Island herd. And that is good news.

▲
Polar bears appear and then disappear along the ice edges and open shore of northwestern Alaska, hunting seals.

▲
Arctic foxes roam the wild coast of northwestern Alaska.

Nunivak is still a long way from Barrow, a long, hard way unless you have the means to fly. To make the trip by boat would mean cruising northward past one of the world's largest river deltas, that of the Yukon and Kuskokwim rivers, maybe in some of the harshest weather imaginable. Although all of the world's emperor geese winter in the Aleutian Islands, most nest here in the Yukon delta, specifically within the 22-million-acre Yukon Delta National Wildlife Refuge, our largest. Vast as it is, as large as Missouri, much of the delta is a maze of grasses, sedges, sloughs and ponds only a few inches above sea level. In springtime and summer it is also among the world's greatest bird breeding areas and one of the greatest producers of waterfowl in Alaska or anywhere else. Cackling geese, black brant and tundra swans, along with the emperor geese, are the largest of the nesting waterfowl. Millions of shorebirds of many species begin life here each year. Fortunately for the birdlife, it is not a pleasant place for humans. The hordes of mosquitoes that hatch in June are one big reason. Only a few Native American villages exist in the delta area.

Continuing northward is like gradually disappearing into another blue and white world, around Nome and the Seward Peninsula, past Cape Prince of Wales, and through Bering Strait, where Russia (Big Diomede Island) might be visible on occasional sunny days, across the Arctic Circle and into the Chukchi Sea. According to most maps, you are in the Arctic Ocean once you round Cape Lisburne. But this isn't even possible for much of the year because it is covered by the Arctic ice pack. Polar bears roam the pack ice from here to Barrow, at the top of Alaska, and beyond.

The end of our journey from Baja to Barrow is not an enticing place to most humans. The bleak featureless town seems to doze at 20 feet above sea level. The normal daily high temperature during the warmest month, July, is about 44 degrees Fahrenheit. At noon every November 18th, the sun sets and does not reappear until noon on January 24th. On the other hand, the sun never dips below the horizon between May 10th and August 2nd. In other words, there is constant daylight, and temperatures reach the mid-50s at this time of the Arctic year. During this period of 24-hour sunlight, some wildlife may be seen, most of it offshore.

Bowheads are the only large whales found routinely in Arctic waters. They hug shorelines and the edge of the Arctic ice shelf, travel in small groups of four or five; they mate in spring and seem to easily become stranded. They are not difficult to see and identify because, unlike other whales, their back lacks a dorsal fin. Adults might exceed 100 tons in weight. Maybe as many as 2,000 cruise close to the north Alaska coast, virtually the last of a what once was a much larger, more world-wide population. The Inuit of the Barrow region continue to battle for the traditional right to hunt the few surviving bowheads.

A more numerous—but usually less visible—resident of the Alaska north coast is the smaller beluga, or white whale. Males reach 15 feet and weigh more than 3,000 pounds; females are somewhat smaller. Belugas also lack dorsal fins, which would be impediments to movement under the ice. These whales live their entire lives immersed in icy water. Scientists have noticed that during bitter winters, belugas must breathe air as cold as minus 60 degrees Fahrenheit, which is exhaled as a shower of ice. The investigators have also learned that belugas are extremely vocal, traveling and keeping in touch with one another by employing a repertoire of wild sounds that resemble a symphony orchestra tuning up prior to a concert.

We have not yet seen the bowheads and belugas of Barrow ourselves, but we have plans. There is an old saying that "Once you've been to Alaska, you never quite come home again." We have found this, after more than two dozen trips to Alaska's wilderness, an undeniable truth.

Belugas are sometimes present in cold Arctic waters off Point Barrow.

▼

Photography

I cannot imagine a finer, more rewarding life than one spent photographing wildlife and wilderness with an extraordinary wife who shares my enthusiasm. During the 20 or so years during which we worked on *Baja to Barrow*, most days were never long enough. Of course there were disappointments, as when Pacific coastal weather refused to clear, when an old tent leaked during a cold, all-night downpour, or when bears and spawning salmon did not show up at a scheduled time. But mostly the life was plain exhilarating.

We traveled by many different means to obtain these photos. By commercial jet plane and by much slower bush floatplane. On water we wandered via everything from car ferry and rebuilt research vessel to inflatable rubber rafts, sight-seeing and party boats and kayaks. On shore we drove, mostly in our small van, or hiked, rode horseback, snowshoed or cross-country skied. In Hawaii we rode tricycles.

Our cameras were 35mm single lens reflex (SLR) models with (in recent years) motor drives to advance film, and automatic focus capability. I suppose neither of these features is really necessary, but they are extremely helpful to cameramen who have, together, spent a half century exposing film. The motor drive allows the photographer to concentrate on his subject and on composition in the viewfinder without having to advance film with a thumb. The automatic focus is all important to anyone whose vision is less than perfect, and it enables anyone to lock onto an active, moving subject more quickly.

▶

Hallo Bay, Katmai, Alaska.

As often as not, we carry more lenses than may seem necessary. For wildlife photographers, the workhorses are the telephotos. To photograph the least shy or habituated (to people) creatures we use 80-200mm zooms. More often we must use longer telephoto lenses; specifically 300mm (which is six power), 400mm, and 600mm (which is twelve power). A small 1.4X extender carried in a pocket and inserted between the camera and any of those long lenses increases their magnifying power by 40 percent.

The 35mm SLRs are the easiest of all cameras yet devised to carry and use in wildlife photography. They are fairly lightweight, compact, fit comfortably in the hands, and are versatile and reliable in all kinds of weather. Still, problems occur, invariably at the least convenient times. So we always carry spare camera bodies. Since we always work together or very near to one another, all of the cameras are the same and are interchangeable with all of the lenses.

There are great advantages in this working together, not the least of which is the rich, warm companionship. True, there may be a lot of duplication in the results, but just as often the pictures are made from slightly different angles or are taken split seconds apart—enough to make a difference. Two cameras are less likely to be empty of film at some crucial moment—as when giant brown bears are fighting—than is one, although this happens more often than statistics would seem to suggest.

We use very sturdy tripods with the 400mm and 600mm lenses because they are quite heavy and need adequate support. In the field we may not use tripods as often as some other professional photographers because there usually are rocks or tree limbs or backpacks on which to rest and steady the shorter telephotos. We hand-hold everything up to 300mm if the exposure allows a shutter speed of at least 1/250 second.

The question we are most often asked in the field is: "What kind of film do you use?" The answer is color positive, or slide, film, medium speed (ASA-ISO 100) if the day is bright, or fairly fast (ASA-

ISO 200) if the light is poor. We may at times shoot either of these at a faster rating, a technique called "pushing," and have the film processed accordingly.

So much has been written about which film brands are best for wildlife/nature use that it is bewildering. The truth is that almost all of the popular, advertised films will suffice at one time or another. Variables, such as the quality of the light, the vegetation and unique reflective aspects of the scene, as well as that of the subject, at any given time determines which film will render the best, most faithful reproduction. Light quality is a very subtle thing, and I am convinced that no single color film yet developed is best all of the time. During any day's shooting we are likely to use several types of film to cover all the bases.

Some other gear may be equally important as cameras, lenses and film for obtaining good wildlife coverage. You cannot concentrate, for example, if clouds of mosquitoes are driving you mad, as they might along north Pacific shores. So we have repellents handy. Even more easily than it can ruin photographers' spirits, rain can ruin cameras, so we carry foul weather suits for ourselves and plastic coverings for the equipment. It may seem strange in the field, but an umbrella (especially one that can be attached to a tripod) can be one of the most valuable items carried.

Adequate, and by that I mean warm enough, clothing is also essential. We use the layering system when it is practical. Any warm outer jacket should have plenty of pockets. At other times we wear light photographers' vests or belt (fanny) packs to carry film and small items.

▲
Using a tricycle along the airstrip on Tern Island.

▲
Heading into Class IV rapids on the Alsek River.

Footwear may be the most critical item, no matter what the type of photography. If we are required to be in cold water, we wear waterproof hip boots with insulated bottoms. For lengthy walking through wetlands, over-the-knee "irrigation boots" or calf-high "Wellies" are lighter in weight than hip boots. For standing out in the snow or intense cold, we wear heavily insulated, waterproof pacs with thick, absorbent socks. Most often we walk or climb over hard, dry ground, and there are many excellent ankle-high backpacker boots on the market today designed exactly for the purpose.

No matter whether planning a trip or actually en route, we have found a new set of atlases indispensable, and have used them constantly during the writing of this book. We have one set in the office and another in our vehicle. They are the DeLorme maps and atlases (DeLorme Mapping Co., P.O. Box 298, Freeport, Maine 04032. Telephone 207/865-4171).

Whole volumes could be written about stalking and shooting wildlife with a camera. But very few situations we have ever faced were exactly the same as previous ones. Because a frightened or fleeing creature is of absolutely no value to us—and frightening or otherwise disturbing animal photo subjects is to be anyway avoided for ethical reasons—we approach everything from hummingbirds to polar bears slowly and with the greatest caution. Never during decades of photographing along the Pacific Coast have we been threatened, let alone attacked by anything but bees, black flies and mosquitoes. Getting within suitable camera range, when it is possible at all, is a matter of patience and being unhurried. We always watch our subjects for signs of nervousness, and when we see that behavior, we stop. We never directly approach animals, even those that are exposed to people every day in parks and reserves. Instead we move at a shallow angle, back and forth, gradually narrowing the distance. It is a strategy that pays off, resulting in images that often reflect the essence of the creature in its chosen habitat.

▲

Aboard the R.V. (Research Vessel) Waters in Hallo Bay.

◄

Peggy standing among the cardon cactus in Baja.